Embracing Your
Big Fat Ass

LAURA BANKS and
JANETTE BARBER

Embracing Your
Big Fat Ass

An Owner's Manual

ATRIA BOOKS
New York London Toronto Sydney

ATRIA BOOKS

A Division of Simon & Schuster, Inc.
1230 Avenue of the Americas
New York, NY 10020

First Atria Books trade paperback edition June 2008

ATRIA BOOKS and colophon are trademarks of Simon & Schuster, Inc.

For information about special discounts for bulk purchases,
please contact Simon & Schuster Special Sales at
1-800-456-6798 or business@simonandschuster.com.

Designed by Jessica Shatan Heslin, Studio Shatan, Inc.

Manufactured in the United States of America

10 9 8 7 6 5 4 3 2 1

Library of Congress Cataloging-in-Publication Data
Banks, Laura.
   Embracing your big fat ass / by Laura Banks and Janette Barber.—1st ed.
     p. cm.
   1. Weight loss.   2. Body image in women.   3. Buttocks—Humor.
I. Barber, Janette. II. Title.
   RM222.2.B363   2008
   613.2'5—dc22   2008014120

ISBN-13: 978-1-4165-4279-7
ISBN-10:   1-4165-4279-5

To all women with curves. We salute you.

*In Loving Memory
Rowland P. Barber*

Contents

Section II   **Your Life as a Basket Case**

Section III   **Romance and Your Big Fat Ass**

Section IV   **Clothing, Friendship, Shopping, and Other Distractions**

Section V   **A Working Woman with a Waddle**

Section VI Attempted Health and Weight Loss Projects

Section VII Leaving It All Behind

In Conclusion The Art of Masstery

Foreword

by Rosie O'Donnell

I remember one day back on my talk show when I was planning to have my best friend Jackie on the program for the first time. She lived across the street from me in Commack, Long Island. We met when we were three. I was telling the audience about Jackie in my opening monologue and had even dug out some old photos to show on TV the day before she was scheduled. One of the pictures was of me and Jackie, waiting for our dates, all dressed up to go to our high school prom. I hadn't seen that snapshot in a long time and when it came up on-screen I surprised myself by saying out loud, "God I was thin!" Which surprised me because I didn't think of myself as ever being thin growing up. But looking back at teenage me, I saw that I wasn't fat at all! How sad that I missed being thin when I actually was. I don't know what caused me to see fat where there was none.

Maybe it was TV—I'd never be Marcia Brady perfect, maybe it was kids at school, or maybe it was just feeling different and living in a motherless house. I wonder if it would have changed things if I had known what I actually looked like. Did I really just grow up and fulfill the picture of myself that I had inside my head?

I'd always thought I was fat, so that photo was an eye-opener for me. I hadn't understood how disconnected from reality my body image really was. If you can't see yourself, it's hard to accept yourself. That's what I like about this book. It's got a very funny title and some great jokes, but it's really about seeing yourself and accepting yourself and about shedding the shame that society seems to think overweight people deserve.

The older I get the clearer it becomes that being fat or being thin has very little to do with what an individual has to contribute. It's also a reality that fat and thin—like life and death—is always in flux. I can tell you what I weighed five years ago. And I can tell you what I weigh today. But I haven't the remotest idea what I will weigh five years into the future. I could find myself channeling Twiggy or I could be playing Orca in the remake. I don't know. Why on earth would I want to tie my self-worth to something that fluctuates so much?

What I do know is that, during these hypothetical five years, I hope to live a good life and do as much as I can, through my foundation and my Rosie's Broadway Kids program, so that I can make a difference and be involved and active with my own kids and family. Isn't that more important than how much I will weigh?

Fat stands on the last frontier of prejudice. "Fat" is one of the worst things you can call a person. If someone makes you mad enough, even if they're thin you'll call them fat. It's a one-size-fits-all insult. I think it's time to change that conversation. We need to start seeing in ourselves and one another the true person we are each meant to be without getting bogged down by a number on a scale or the size tag in our pants.

When Janette first told me she was writing a book called *Embracing Your Big Fat Ass* with her coauthor, Laura Banks, I laughed out loud. I am a comic—I believe anything can be made better or at least more palatable with laughter. This book has humor to lighten the load along with some surprisingly touching stories and insights about living fat in America. I applaud the start of the new conversation.

Just love yourself and your friends and your family and then do the very best you can. That's enough. Peace out.

The Birth of the B-FABs
(Big Fat Ass Babes)

What's in a Word?

LB: Co-Founding Member Confessional

If the name of this book offends you in any way, Janette and I are not sorry. We are writing this book to make friends, to meet many of you, and have some great tailgate parties on the road, but there is simply no other title that would work for this book. "Embracing Your Big Fat Behind?" "Embracing Your Big Fat Bottom?" Maybe in reviews of this book in magazines and on TV our title will look like this: *Embracing Your Big Fat A***. Maybe they'll try to bleep us when we use the word on the local news in Tallahassee. Janette loves the word *ass*, among other more descriptive terms. By using a profanity—granted, on the lower end of the profanity spectrum, in our opinion—we give the book the "bite" it needs. That's why the word works. It has a bit of snarl to it.

There was an actual event that led to this title. It came about in the summer of 2002. A friend of mine, Carol, came storming into my apartment, slammed my front door, and walked into my kitchen. Carol is a beautiful woman, very turned out with gorgeous designer clothes, a luxury sports car, and a fancy Fifth Avenue job in New York City as an executive secretary. She even has a secretary. She's a secretary with a secretary. Anyway, Carol goes to the gym at least five days per week and has a great body to show for it. Her apartment overlooks the Hudson River with mirrors on the entire wall in the living room reflecting magnificent water views. It's breathtakingly gorgeous. Bottom line: she's a perfectionist in many areas of her life so it couldn't have been easy for her when she finally broke down, looked me square in the eyes, and after a brilliantly crafted pause said, "I give up. I just have to accept the fact that I have a fat ass." I laughed so hard I thought I would pass out. I felt like I had been hit in the ass by a bolt of lightning.

Another factor in the equation was that when Carol zapped me with this declaration of resignation and acceptance of her ass, I was reading the book *Embraced by the Light*, by Betty Eadie. The book is about Betty almost dying and what she experienced while moving toward "the light," being lifted above mortal concerns into a safe place of peace, understanding, and acceptance. That's when I got it; having a fat ass is like having a near-death experience. You just have to keep breathing and move toward the light, only in this case it's the light coming from the refrigerator.

Fast-forward to 2006 and I still hadn't done anything with this title. I finally worked up the courage to call Janette, fearful that she would think I was crazy to want to write an entire book about my rear end. But she was perfect for the project because she's a hysterically funny writer, and I also knew she had wrestled with her ass in the past. No one would be more capable than Janette to wax poetic on this very weighty subject. When I called her on the phone and told her the title, I had never heard her laugh so hard in my life. I thought that was a good sign.

We're attacking one of life's biggest jokes, one of its deepest injustices—that constant pain in our hearts about not being pretty enough on the outside to find love for ourselves on the inside. Janette and I are not anthropologists. We hold no degrees in science or nutrition. We hold our own self-proclaimed Doctorate in Self-Loathing with a Minor in Using Food for Emotional Control. We've graduated. This is our thesis. It's more than jokes. This is the story of our asses. We've included our real-life confessionals so that you can see how we became who we are.

It's our mission to spread the word: Love your asses. Love yourself. There is no reason to be unhappy anymore. Life should be lived as if it were a near-death experience every day, 'cause if it were, would you really be that concerned about your ass?

Embracing Your Big Fat Ass

Most of us hate our behinds. It takes very little to make you feel like you have a Big Fat Ass (BFA). You can be talking about five pounds, ten pounds, twenty pounds, or a bubble butt and you self-qualify. Life is too short to be limited by your own ass. All of us need to forgive and forget what we look like from the rear. Who cares what it looks like as long as it stays in the background? What you can't see can't hurt you.

We are all the butt of some very funny butt jokes, mostly delivered by ourselves while trying on that pair of pants from just last year that now compresses all the oxygen out of our bodies. Give them to the Salvation Army and take the tax deduction. (With what you save you can buy a nice comforting cupcake.) If you can get rid of your last boyfriend, you can get rid of those stupid pants—both just took up space in your bedroom! (Janette insists we insert her theory here that there could be something in the air or the water—probably released by the government—that is shrinking all our clothes. Believe it if you want. Denial is a very powerful tool.)

Give Yourself a Pat on the Ass

Give yourself a big pat on the ass for picking up this book. That means that you are willing to admit that you are obsessed with your Big Fat Ass. You are over the hump, above the hurdle, and will never ever have to submit to wearing a girdle. Of course you want to lose weight but you're ready to face the fact that your backside may or may not be getting any smaller any day in the near future. We got embarrassed about it and then we got depressed about it and then we got over it—over coveting all the perfect asses in magazines, on TV, and in the movies. We've finally acknowledged that it's going to take way too much work and we are just too darned tired to make our asses look like that.

We've come to the conclusion that the time is now to embrace our Big Fat Asses. There is no reason to let your butt be your bane. Let your BFA be part of you instead of trying to pretend it's sandbags hanging off your belt. The only one you are fooling is yourself so break out that Big Fat Ass and revel in it. Join a nudist colony if you want to. Who cares what anyone else thinks? Although she still proudly sports a BFA, Janette has lost over a hundred pounds. You should see her in a bathing suit. When she runs she looks like a lava lamp. Be brave. Wear a thong. (Be aware that tiny thongs can be hazardous to the prodigious posterior so be sure to wear a bright color. It will make the thong easier to spot should a trip to the emergency room prove to be necessary.)

The most important thing is to not get sidetracked by think-ing that all of your dozens and dozens of dieting attempts didn't succeed. Just because you weigh sixteen and a half pounds more now than you did before you started trying to lose weight in the first place does not mean you have failed. To quote Thomas Ed-ison when he was working on inventing the lightbulb, "I have not failed. I've discovered ten thousand things that won't work." It's all just process. You are processing your ass. That process will, in all likelihood, never end so why not embrace that too? We see no reason to be unhappy. It makes us want to ask the question: Why can't we all just be friends with our asses?

The point is that we're really happy you bought this book. On the upside, if you're like us you're a good eater so you're probably not hungry. Neither are we. (Could somebody please pass the chips?) Welcome aboard and move your fat ass over. Make room for some friends and cozy up to *Embracing Your Big Fat Ass*. (P.S. There is a crack going down the middle of this book. That is not specifically designed to be funny. All books have a crack going down the middle.)

Your Uniquely Fat Situation

Having a BFA is a deeply personal experience. What consti-tutes a BFA varies. Why, we know a woman who is always in a fit about her longitudinous BFA, yet if you saw her walk by, you'd say, "Oh look, there goes a button-butt." This is what proves Einstein's theory of relativity. In spite of his hairstyle, that man really was a genius. What is a BFA to one B-FAB (Big Fat Ass Babe) might not be a BFA to another but they both deserve our respect, darn it.

Big Fat Ass Babes are also Beautiful Fat Ass Babes. Let's just accept our asses and get on with our lives. It's like your Visa bill. Why worry about it when you know you'll never pay it off even if you live to be a hundred? Your ass is like that. It will always be with you—like debt, with interest doubling daily.

The Lost Art of the Big Fat Ass

A big, beautiful behind has been an inspiration to some of the greatest painters of all time: Degas, Matisse, Delacroix, and Renoir, to name a few. These men knew that there is nothing more sensual, more inviting, and more romantic than the soft curves of a big round tushy. They reveled in the sensuality of the not-so-delicate curves of their portly models. Renoir is famous for his babes with asses that took up most of the canvas— fat asses stepping into the bath, stepping out of the bath, looking into the mirror and polishing their asses with towels. He must have gone through many tubes of paint to finish one mammoth butt cheek. In fact, one historian (who's dead now) noted that Renoir painted so many fat asses that he once passed out from the paint fumes. But it was well worth it since that was back in the time when fat asses were hot. We need to take a lesson from fat ass painters everywhere, they who glorify the rotund, and be reminded that in other centuries our BFAs were worshipped and adored. What happened? Did we lose our minds? How did we forget that we're beautiful?

What If We're Confused About How We Feel About Our BFAs?

Think of something you love very much but you're ashamed of it anyway—like your husband, your son, and your pet that always wets on the neighbors when they visit. You don't love them any less because you're ashamed of them. Well, that's the same approach you need to take with your rump. It's just like anything else you suffer extreme humiliation from. We want to discourage you from putting all your time and energy into hating your behind—that thing that follows you around every day like a gosh-darn freight train. Know that the self-loathing you have toward your backside will never go away. We want you to embrace the hate and become one with your panty size.

This book can become an important resource. For example, we might give you great suggestions on how to hide your ass in a tight pair of black jeans with sweaters, scarves, plants, and common household appliances. We could even let you know the pets to choose to best accessorize your thighs. (We know a woman, poor thing, who unwittingly sat on her toy poodle. They didn't find Fluffy for three weeks! Of course he kept barking but it was misdiagnosed as wind. A lesson for us all.) The most important thing that you will learn from us is that you are not alone.

How Can You Be Sure You Have a BFA?

The first sign is that you have bought this book and that you are laughing. Most B-FABs have a great sense of humor but they do not enjoy having other people laugh *at* them. Now *with* them?

You go girl! True B-FABs have already figured out that we are starting off this book with humor to make you like us and to distract from our asses. Isn't that what you do at parties? Isn't that the B-FAB way? We'll get down to the serious stuff later. After we've drawn you in. Aren't we clever?

All doubts about whether or not you have a BFA can be eliminated if you fit the following criteria: If your BFA is truly gigantic you will notice that the top of your butt, just below your waist, has formed a shelf. This is annoying in some ways and handy in others. For example, your clothing can get stuck on your ass shelf and expose something horrific, like the backs of your thighs. On the other hand, after a movie, you can still find popcorn when you get home. If you have a shelf on your body, let's face it—you're furniture. You're probably a B-FAB. (If you don't have a shelf and have no idea what we're talking about but you can't lose that last nagging five pounds you can still qualify—it's all a state of mind.)

If you are still questioning whether your ass is truly a fat ass, there is also the classic BFA sign: Cheek Spillage. You recognize it. If you sit down, say in your baby-doll pajamas, on a hard kitchen chair and if a generous amount of flesh falls over the outside edge, you're in the club. Many people even experience spillage while fully clothed. It's even worse on a wooden chair in an open-air restaurant and especially if the day happens to be breezy. You could experience Butt Flap. Like sheets hanging on the clothesline, whipping in the wind—only it's your spillage. We imagine that it would make an alarming sound, something like a goose that you've hung out on the line during a nor'easter. Maybe it would be better if we skip all that and just avoid restaurants with those little tiny seats.

Quiz: How Big Is Your Fat Ass?

Do you:

1. Knock over freestanding displays in stores?

2. Often lose things in your pants?

3. Wear long shirts over everything you own including evening gowns?

4. Hate the idea of a rearview mirror even if it's just in the car?

5. Refuse to date a skinny ass man, convinced you'll look bigger in comparison?

6. Refuse to date a skinny ass man, convinced you might sit on him and kill him?

Score. Count your number of yeses

1–3   Your ass isn't that big yet, but don't worry, it will be.

3–5   Definitely a fat ass but still fits through turnstiles.

Over 5 Enjoy it, wiggle it, let it flap in the wind. You have a Big Fat Ass.

Your Butt as an Integral Part of Your Life

There are many people who think they would prefer to have no butt at all. This is less practical than you might expect. We'll spare you the obvious jokes about how difficult it would be for them to sit, and go straight to stressing how bad your jeans would look if you had no ass at all. Just a hollow underneath your belt. Is that any better? No it is not. Suddenly you're getting some little glint of *gratitude* about what that nice lard unit is doing for you. You need your butt and your butt needs you. This is what life is all about.

Let's Review: Accepting Your BFA Made Easy!

Reach a truce with your BFA in record time with two easy steps:

Step 1: Welcome your BFA. Stop fighting it.

Stop buying clothes that don't fit as an "incentive." Take the picture of the model off the refrigerator. This is all psychologically combative behavior. Stop rejecting yourself and judging yourself and measuring your self-worth by your BFA because, quite frankly, you're going to lose. Instead say to your ass, "Welcome to my life—all I ask is that you stay behind me." Let your ass alone. Make a deal with your ass. It can do whatever it wants back there as long as it doesn't expect you to react to it.

Step 2: Remember to laugh.

In the words of Elsa Maxwell, "Laugh at yourself first, before anyone else can." Laughter lightens up the situation and makes it easier to face. Throughout this book we will say outrageous things, mocking things, shocking things. Please note: We are being funny. We are defusing emotions with humor. We are, in short, making ourselves feel better. We think it will be great if it makes you feel better, too. Really, we think that would be good, so please drop everything and go send our publishers an e-mail telling them that you like us so far. Remember the old saying: If your ass doesn't kill you, it will make you stronger!

Born to Be a B-FAB

JB: Co-Founding Member Confessional

ome people are born with BFAs, but others have one thrust upon them. In my opinion I was such a one because, up until first grade, I was totally normal. (In this case where I am pairing the concepts of "Janette" and "normal," I am, clearly, speaking exclusively about my weight and not my mental health.) What with being abandoned by my mother as an infant and growing up in a two-hundred-year-old farmhouse in the middle of 148 acres with a nut cake father (bless his heart) and no neighbors in sight, no relatives, no friends, no TV—the word *normal* would not apply to any other aspects of my personality. By the time I was seven years old, in second grade, I already weighed 115 pounds. By the eighth grade I weighed 200½ pounds. I weighed 250 at fourteen. Have you figured it out? I was a normal weight as long as I was alone.

As soon as I met people I began to swell. Janette doesn't play well with others.

Many of my therapists (What? How many therapists have *you* had? If the answer is none, for God's sake find one. You must be a raving lunatic) have conjectured that my parents weren't my biggest problem—which, under the circumstances seems rather shocking. My biggest issues appear to have started up when I, to my dismay, first encountered "other children." Yuck. I didn't like them and I had no intention whatsoever of wasting time with them. For whatever reason, this made me stand out as, umm, an oddball. Go figure.

When I decided to start grade school I had a very definite plan. (Of course it was my decision. If you think I have ever in my life done anything I didn't want to do, then you don't really know me yet.) I was going there to learn to read. I couldn't wait. I loved books. I memorized the books my great-aunt Martie read to me and then pretended to read them out loud to whoever would listen. For a while my father thought he had a prodigy on his hands until he realized I couldn't actually be reading be-cause I was turning the pages at the wrong times. So, reading was what I went to school to learn but the miserable teachers had other ideas. They wanted us to take time away from the important work of learning to read and instead walk around the room in a circle singing, in unison, some idiot song while Mrs. Gagnon played the piano. Puhlease! I sulked, obsessing over the wasted time since I still hadn't mastered the F'ing alphabet. Then there was drawing (give me a break) and math (don't in-sult me) and—every single day—they forced us to have not one but two recess periods. I was incensed. The second recess was worse than the first because the teacher made the kids play games together that involved standing in a circle and holding hands. *I think not! I'm perfectly fine here by the wall with my arms crossed and my head down staring at my feet. I will NOT hold your hand; go away.* I wouldn't speak to anyone unless it specifically supported my goal, which was, have I mentioned . . . learning to read.

I had a first-grade teacher who clearly fits into the above-admonished group of people who have never had therapy. Not only did she tell us there was no Santa (*Shocking! No! Could it be true?*), but every time we had to make some stupid craft project to take home to our mothers this teacher would announce to the class, "And for Janette and Lorraine [another little girl in the class] I'll write FATHER on the board because they don't *have* any mothers." Every time this happened it was like crushed glass in my eye, rubbing in the reality of my abandonment. Lorraine's mother at least had had the common decency to die. Mine had, to quote my poor, sad father, run away: "Your mother ran away."

It was a criminal divorce. Adultery was a crime in those days. For years after she was gone my father would drill my sister and me about what to say in court if our mother, who was now named "Mrs. Willy," ever tried to get us. (" 'I want to stay with Daddy. Daddy.' I said it. Okay . . . 'I want to stay with Daddy; I don't want to go with Mrs. Willy.' ") My sister and I used to worry a lot about what would happen if this horrible harpy who we barely knew ever tried to retrieve us, but, in fact, she didn't and I never saw her again.

I did, on the upside, learn to read. Really, really well. I am a good reader. All my therapists have also pointed out that, when I was a kid and when I was in emotional crisis, I turned to food (obvious) and that I ate specifically to be fat (less obvious to me) because I needed the fat to protect me. The trick is that as an adult I no longer needed as much protection so was able to lose the hundred pounds. But apparently I *do* still need this extra twenty-five pounds of thighs and ass. (I don't care so don't nag me to lose it. Get off my back. That's why God gave everybody an ass—so you can go obsess about your own and leave mine alone. Hrmph.)

Knowing that it serves a purpose makes me like my Big Fat Ass so much more. My good old butt. My life partner. It was there for me when I needed it. It was there for me in the beginning and will be there in the end. It's been so unfair of me to hate my ass or myself for having such a big one. Of course I'm constantly trying to keep it at bay so that I don't have to add a guest cottage to my house to accommodate it, but that's no reason to feel bad about myself. It's what I do. Some people like to hike, others enjoy crafting. I fight with my ass. Life is good.

Self-Image—
A Snapshot from Behind

How you feel about yourself and how you feel about your ass are inextricably connected. If you hate your ass you hate yourself. When you fight with your ass you are fighting with yourself. You're going to have to take you and your ass to couples therapy. The first thing you'll have to understand is: THIS IS NOT ALL ABOUT YOU. Your ass has a point of view, too. Your Big Fat Ass has been there watching your back for very many years. It's time to give a little back to your ass. It's time to embrace it. It's time to become a self-accepting, self-actualized B-FAB. Who said "happy" is for other people?

You Are Who You Think You Are

What you think of yourself is often *so* much more powerful than what others think of you. Janette learned this in her mid-thirties. She had been significantly overweight since childhood and as it turns out, no one was harder on her than she was herself. This became very apparent after she had lost a lot of weight in 1990.

Janette, a stand-up comic at the time, was riding to upstate New York for a gig with fellow comic Mike Sweeney (the long-time head writer on *Late Night with Conan O'Brien*). Janette had lost fifty pounds since she had last seen Mike so it was of course a topic of conversation. Mike asked Janette how it felt to lose so much weight that some people she knew didn't even recognize her. Janette, with this weight loss still fresh in her mind, was, as usual, riding a broom. She was mad. She was sick of it. She told Mike how much it bothered her that people who hadn't spoken to her before were all kinds of friendly now. She was even mad that comedy bookers who hadn't used her before were now offering her club dates. Most people would have just listened to her but Mike Sweeney is a better man than that. Even though they were no more than acquaintances, instead of thinking about his own discomfort, he decided to tell her the truth. He said, "Well, Janette, I'm sure that's true . . . but when you were really fat you were so down on yourself all the time that you were kind of embarrassing to be around." That hit Janette like a stick in the stomach. All this time she had thought people didn't like her because of her weight . . . but as it turns out it was her personality! What a shock. And what a gift! That was a life-changing moment. That's when she discovered that she was the biggest influence in her own life.

Self-Esteem and Your Ass

It is important to realize that you are in complete control of your self-esteem, such as it is. If you have ever read a Dale Carnegie book or attended a motivational seminar of any kind—including "Organizing Your Closet!"—then you know that your attitude about a thing determines its effect on your life. It's the same with your ass. It's not about what other people think of it. It's about what you think about what other people think about what you think about your ass. Use visualization techniques to reprogram your mind to see your fat ass as the beautiful extension of you that it truly is (even if you do hate it most of the time).

For example, see this in your mind as clearly as if you were watching a movie. Imagine yourself out on a date with a glamorous, exciting, handsome man who you think is very likely to be "the one" even though you hardly know him. Clearly visualize that your ass, regardless of the fact that it's so huge it looks like a bustle, doesn't get in the way of his adoring gaze. Right there, once you can see that, end, cut—it's a wrap. This technique can help you achieve anything in the world you could ever want—except calorie-free s'mores. You can visualize yourself at the dreaded family barbecue in those bright red Bermuda shorts, only this time it's different. You're having fun and no one, including yourself, is judging your ass. You can visualize a job interview where the entire office is decorated with Renoir prints and by the end of the interview you not only have the job, you have an employee parking space and you're engaged. See it however you want. Normally you're filling your head up with "I hate myself and my ass is fat and I'm never going to get what I want." And then you *wonder* why you aren't happy! Hmmm.

Low Self-Esteem and Its Dire Effect on Your Bum

In the dictionary it should say: **ass**—see LOW SELF-ESTEEM. But we say a poor self-image is just like your ass. As long as you have it, you might as well learn to live with it. Once you understand that it's only your own head talking when you're having all these negative thoughts about yourself, then you can just write them off as low self-esteem and stop believing in them! It's a bum rap. (Isn't that a sandwich?)

Low self-esteem is really just plain sad. It's this weird choice we make to hate ourselves because other people have said mean things about us. Say we're in line at the minimart buying a Snickers bar so we don't have a blackout before we get home to our insulin. Someone in line behind us says something like "Lay off the candy." Why do *we* feel horrible shame as if *we* did something wrong? He's the Shallow Hal who probably has a very nervous skinny girlfriend. Besides . . . you're in line. He's seeing your ass from behind. It's *his* problem.

In psychological terms this is called an interject. It's a negative thought implanted in your mind by some jerk at the Piggly Wiggly that you then adopt as your own belief. So stop that. Low self-esteem makes it hard for B-FABs to stand up for ourselves. Next time that happens buy a couple of extra Chunky bars and give them to the name-caller as a gift. Tell him to stick them where the sun don't shine. Enjoy your Snickers.

Each Time You Say Yes and Succeed Your Self-Esteem Grows

There is only one word and it is *yes*. The truth is, there is nothing you can't achieve as long as you're willing and able to do the work to get there. No one knows what she can do until she tries! Pretty much anything is up for grabs except for jobs that make you squeeze through very, very tight passageways—like cave diving. Cave diving is probably hard if you have a Big Fat Ass. We don't do it and aren't interested even if somebody sends us a free cave-diving trip. (And, believe us, we very rarely turn down a free trip.) But, ugh. What if we were down there and the cave got tight?

There are lots of things you can do that can make you feel great. Too many of us B-FABs tend to isolate ourselves rather than going out where we face the fear of thin people among us saying mean things about our asses. In fact, the very best way to make your boring-ass life take a quantum leap is to just accept every invitation that comes along for the next thirty years. Why are you staying home? Your ass isn't any smaller when you're alone. If we would let ourselves go dancing or hiking or to a gym we'd actually feel better and might even tighten up that glorious Airstream motor coach we call our derrière, but no. We think we deserve to sit home and have no fun at all. Stop feeling so guilty.

For all we know, round about the year 2525 they will have whole history books talking about the time on earth when the fat plague struck. No one could understand it until they realized that the government was releasing a secret fat gas so that people would have health problems, so that the drug companies could make more money. We don't know. Anything could be true, so why should we hate ourselves over it? We all got dealt a different ass in the big card game of life. We've found that if we just play the ass we're dealt we can have very wonderful lives.

TESTIMONIAL

B-FAB Lucy

I like asses. I don't know why. I just like them. I am always look-ing for the next great ass or a funny-looking ass to make my-self feel better about mine. When I was about twenty-four years old I had a great ass. It had this great beauty mark on my left cheek and one day I noticed it starting to hurt when I sat down. So I took a mirror and put it to my rear view and noticed my beauty mark was growing.

I became worried and sought out my dermatologist, who said I had a melanoma that had to be removed. I was scared I was going to die of skin cancer on my ass so I did the only thing I could do: schedule surgery. That was traumatic, as you could imagine. (Oh, I forgot to mention that I had spent the bulk of that year naked in a tanning salon. The doctor said that's how the melanoma happened. Warning: stay out of tan-ning salons.) The surgery itself was painless but strange. There I lay, nude from the waist down on a surgical table with a mir-ror in hand and my bare bottom exposed for all the world to see. The doctor explained to me that he was going to give me an injection and then I would go numb. So he did and I felt nothing. He pulled down a light and a ruler and began to draw a line and then he took measurements and he took pictures, and all I could do is wonder what he would do with the photos when he was done. He began to tell me how deep he was going to go, but that I wouldn't feel a thing. I began to worry—what was he really doing down there? Then he started stitch-ing and I knew he was done. He rubbed the incision with ointment and put a bandage on it and sent me home with a "doughnut" so that I could sit. It was very uncomfortable and took a few weeks to heal. I have gotten over not being able to wear a thong on a beach, which I had done before the surgery; now I just wear one in private. The scar has faded. It's been fifteen years and to this day I love my ass. You would too if you'd almost lost part of yours.

Some People Seem to Feel Victimized by Their BFAs

We have heard many a B-FAB friend bemoaning how much happier they think their lives would be if they hadn't been saddled with a BFA. They may feel that life is harder for them. They may think they want an easy way out. They might not think that that Big Fat Ass is benefiting them in any way. Be honest. Our asses have done a lot for us. They symbolize hours and hours in a near coma from eating two entire half-gallon containers of Baskin-Robbins and a bag of Fig Newtons. They mean a sausage pizza scarfed while watching *American Idol* instead of thinking about the promotion you didn't get. It's a great excuse for just about anything—I don't have a boyfriend because I'm fat, I don't have that dress because I'm fat, I didn't get that job because I'm fat.

You might be somebody totally different if you didn't have a BFA. You might be some snotty skinny ass femme that has no compassion or real depth. (Not that we are being judgmental, because we're not. We never are. We're just saying. Some of those bony babes act superior and outright mean. That's because they're hungry. Somebody throw them a sandwich.) There's a lot you can learn by facing down your obstacles.

Janette has a favorite story that her great-aunt Martie used to tell her as a kid. For decades Janette has quoted it to people whenever they complain about how hard something is to do. Here it is now for you.

Story of the Milk Cans

Once upon a time, in some Denmark-like country in the far north, there was a group of little boys who were out being a bunch of hooligans and they did something to destroy an old farmer's wagon. The farmer saw what they'd done and he came running out, shaking his fist, telling them that they had destroyed his wagon and it was his only way to take his milk to market. If he didn't take the milk to market he'd have no money and he and his poor old wife would starve. But the nasty bunch of hooligan boys just yelled out, "Oh, who cares about you old man!"

All except one who felt guilty and who said to the others, "You know we really shouldn't have done that. That was wrong. We should take turns carrying his milk to market ourselves until the wagon can be fixed." But his friends all said, "No, we won't do that. He can't make us." And they also wouldn't help because they were all training for the big marathon that happened in the town every year and that time in the morning was when they were all going to run together.

Our boy was also supposed to train for the marathon with all the others but he couldn't live with what he'd done without doing something to make it right. So every day he got up at 5 AM and while the others were out with their coaches in their running outfits he had a huge harness around him holding a big wooden pack with two twenty-five pound cans of milk side by side. He trudged the five miles to market and then ran back as best he could with the empties every day.

The day before the marathon was also the day the wagon was finally fixed, so our boy was free to go compete with all the other boys who had been training every single day. The starting gun went off and he zoomed ahead. He was so used to carrying the heavy milk cans that, released from their weight, he felt like he was flying. Because his daily run had been so much more difficult than that of the other boys who had been practicing in their gym shorts, he easily out-distanced everyone.

It's the same thing with your ass. Think of what you've learned from it! Think about how much more compassion you have for other people. Think about how sensitive we are to other people who have been tormented by others. Think about how much nicer we B-FABs are than all those less fortunate, naturally thin people! We are definitely stronger. We have to be. The emotional luggage in our backside weighs a ton.

Be Kind to Your Behind

Now that you have put everything in perspective and understand everything your ass has done for you, love it! Remember: love is a decision. Make a decision to love your big beefy butt unconditionally, no matter how much humiliation it causes you or how many other-people's-entrées it sweeps off tables as you try to get out of those cramped little New York restaurant tables—not that that's ever happened to us. But we do think that there should be a law preventing tables from being only six inches apart. Condiments and sauces get swept off your own table by your luxurious gut and the strangers to your right have to grip their entrées and lean like Pisa. It's enough to make you want to pack a sandwich and sit on a park bench. Imagine that your ass is your cat and never treat your ass worse than you'd treat Felix. (We are going under the assumption here that you love your cat slavishly, as all cats deserve. If you do not love your cat or are mean to your cat please contact us through our website at www.EmbracingYourBigFatAss.com so we can have you tracked down and arrested. Thanks so much.)

Love your ass even if it becomes like a deranged, feral child hanging off the back of your spine. When you are unkind to your boinga-boinga it tends to severely increase your appetite, making your rump likely to grow bigger and baggier as if to insulate itself from you and all your nastiness. Turn the tables by accepting your ass and appreciating it.

It's All My Mother's Fault

LB: Co-Founding Member Confessional

My mother, God rest her soul, stood only five feet, two and three-quarters inches tall. She'd often brag about that last three-fourths of an inch. By the eighth grade, I stood five feet eleven. I was a giant oversized thing. I towered over my mother and everybody else. My height was my brand of BFA pain and suffering. (Notice here how the BFA can take on allegorical significance and be stretched to signify any kind of humiliation.) I was so tall it hurt. I towered over boys at school. I was taller than my brothers, my dad, my teachers, my girlfriends . . . and my pants.

The mean kids called me the Jolly Green Giant. It felt worse than it sounds. In the hope of appearing more petite I developed terrible posture. As an adolescent I resembled a tall turtle character from some black-and-white Disney cartoon. My chest was concave. I was never popular because I was too big to fit in. Cheerleaders fit in. I loathed those insipid girls with their perfectly petite bodies and perky breasts emblazoned with the school logo, jumping up and down and and satisfying every schoolboy's dreams. They could lift one another up into the air, do spins, and wear matching outfits. I looked nothing like them. I particularly hated the head cheerleader. I tried to imagine how she got that title. I hated my plus-sized body parts even more than I hated them. I knew deep down . . . that there was just too much of me to twirl.

My mom had the petite thing going on without even trying. She'd tell me not to feel bad about my size ten feet because Jackie Kennedy had size ten feet, too. I didn't really get what the First Lady's feet had to do with my feet, but I went along with her. My mother loved anything to do with Jackie: her sunglasses, her purses, her figure, her feet, and her husband.

According to my memory, my mother's strange eating habits began to emerge around this time. I can't call it an eating disorder because that would weird out my dad, who's still alive, and I don't even know if it's true. All I can say—and this is a matter of fact—is that my mother got horribly thin. I knew deep down that it was a control issue and that so many aspects of her life were out of control—her teenage children, her marriage, and the fact that she felt extremely trapped living in Kansas. My mom was a New York City born-and-raised babe, who, when she married my dad, got transplanted to Kansas City, Kansas, which was the beginning of the end for her. Gwen was a brilliant portrait artist and poet. Her art remained primarily unexpressed to anyone but me and her sister, Gloria. I'd find scribbles of beautiful poems on notepads in her dresser and exquisitely drawn charcoal portraits of John F. Kennedy, Dwight D. Eisenhower, Abraham Lincoln, and other good-looking men. For the most part, she kept all of her creativity inside herself, rarely painting and writing, so she could focus on the fears of day-to-day living. Eventually, in what appeared to be a final act of desperation, her dress size became her obsession. Clearly, something was wrong with my mother.

I was in my teens standing in our kitchen in Prairie Village the first time I saw her make her favorite snack—fake pizza. This snack was to become the staple of her existence. Everything seemed to revolve around making this flat and crispy treat.

Recipe for the Gwendolyn Banks Melba Toast Cheese Thingy

Melba toast
low-fat American cheese
Hunt's tomato Sauce

Put the cheese and the tomato sauce on top of the cracker and place it in the toaster oven. (Be careful not to light the house on fire—the cheese tends to bubble and then promptly burst into flames.) Take it out of the oven while crying a little bit for no apparent reason. Eat this for breakfast, lunch, and dinner. (Have a bottle of wine.)

My concerns about my mother's Melba Toast Cheese Thingies started to grow as her silhouette started to shrink. I started to lose my best friend. We stopped having our amazing conversations about life and movies, makeup and boys that lasted until the middle of the night. Her desires to feel in control of something (food) and to look like our modern-day Victoria Beckham outweighed her desire to be with me. Or so it seemed. Mom started to lose muscle mass and, over time, mental clarity while suffering from some disease I cannot name, anorexia, which was an offshoot of another disease I can name, agoraphobia. (That's when you're afraid to leave the house.) Eventually, she was all skin and bones lying on her bed reading the biographies of first ladies.

Anorexia is not a beauty move. You lose your hair and teeth. Your skin prematurely ages and you basically start to dry up from malnutrition. Forget any sex drive or drive for anything other than showing the world that you are in charge . . . of killing yourself.

It seems sad that life can come to a point where the only way to feel some sense of control is to stop allowing nutrients into your body. My mom was losing her life. I thought this was something that my eccentric mother did and that no other mothers ever did, but then I read in a magazine that anorexia is an epidemic among older and younger women alike. I guess my mom wasn't someone to be ashamed of after all. She just wanted to forget the fact that she wasn't Jackie Kennedy.

As I matured I started to carry around extra weight and my mother was obviously disappointed. At holiday gatherings at my brother's house in Denver she'd suggest I cut back on the stuffing and gravy or try other calorie-cutting recipe tricks such as lettuce on a plate. I was scared by her disorder. I craved being more petite and more thin but not at the expense of my life. It didn't really matter to me that I was slightly heavy. I refused to listen to her; I was concerned that I might become anorexic—frightened of a fork and its contents. The pendulum dipped in the other direction for me—never watching what I ate until I got fat and sick with irritable bowel syndrome.

I wish I had figured out at an earlier age that I am not my mother.

In fact, to this day, I always want to eat. There. I said it. I also admit that I blame my mom in some not-so-subtle way, and at the same time I see how mean and absurd that is. Perhaps, having now acknowledged the complexity of my emotions, I can get on with a happier life. If you want to try this at home, here's how. Step one: blame your parents for everything. Step two: realize you're blaming them for everything. Step three: forgive them and yourself for being such a judgmental jerk. Once you are whole and complete with the parent-blame game, you can go on and acknowledge other subsets of people in your life you enjoy playing this with . . . say for instance, men.

Lastly, I've never actually tried the Melba Toast Cheese Thingy. In my mom's honor I will eat one very soon. I will eat it—and then I will eat . . . something else, like maybe some clam fritters. Then I'll go out and buy some heels and be proud of every oversized inch of me.

TESTIMONIAL

B-FAB Dale

My body image is finally not an issue. I'm nearly forty-two years old and it's taken me what feels like a lifetime to be proud, happy, and comfortable in my own skin. I was raised in a family where the primary focus was weight and beauty. If we weren't a size two, we were told we needed to lose weight. Unfortunately, this resulted in a long struggle with food and body image. What I've learned is that being overweight or thin isn't the issue. It's how I define myself. It's making a choice every morning not to have my value and self-worth contingent upon the number on the scale. (And I threw out the f%#king scale! That was so liberating.) I have mistreated and taken this body for granted . . . however, it forgave me and gave me the gift of creating a life—my own beautiful baby—and for this reason alone I love my body and celebrate being a woman.

Big Beautiful Fat Ass Babe Society

(It's About Time!)

We've had it. There appears to be a support group for pretty much everything and everybody—except people who are tormented by their asses. That seems pretty darned significant to us and just more proof that the thin people among us are probably plotting something nefarious that includes no snacks whatsoever. This is why we, Laura Banks and Janette Barber, have decided to become the co-founding charter members of the Big Fat Ass Babe Society, aka the Beautiful Fat Ass Babe Society. Both names are accurate so you can use them interchangeably depending on your mood.

We've decided to turn our negative obsession into a celebration. We invite you to join our movement. Here's all you have to do: Call up or e-mail your girlfriends who also eat food and say something like "Are you sick and tired of being sick and tired of your ass?" If the answer is "Yes I am," then you've begun to build your very own local chapter of the Big Fat Ass Babe (B-FAB) Society. Now both of you can reach out to other B-FAB friends, old and new, and get them to join your local chapter. B-FABs are fed up with obsessing over the size of their nonhourglass figures. Meet your fellow B-FABs for dinner one night a week to *celebrate* your ass. Remember, this is not a *weight loss* club; this is a *weight love* group. It is your own B-FABulous group. It's a hip, beautiful, you've-got-it-going-on-no-matter-what-your-size society. Load your butts up with tattoos, streamers, and glitter. Take pictures of your group and your BFAs. Send them in to www.EmbracingYourBigFatAss.com so we can see and love and celebrate your asses, too! (Don't worry, we won't publish them without your permission.)

The B-FAB Agenda

◈ Stop letting our asses rule our universe.

◈ Understand, finally, that we are as smart, as pretty, as sexy, and as deserving as any show dog.

◈ Go out and get exactly what we want out of life. (More pie.)

◈ Get a break from our neighbors, jobs, houses, lives.

◈ Get away from our husbands and kids.

◈ Remind ourselves that what *we* want is important, too.

◈ Get drunk and talk about everybody we went out with in college.

✧ Know that life is about more than VPL (Visible Panty Line).

The point of the B-FAB Society is to create an atmosphere where you can celebrate accepting yourself exactly as you are. As a group you'll create a safe place to share your stories as we have and to find solace in each other's ups and downs. A B-FAB meeting is a noncritical environment where you can wear shorts without worrying about your fat thighs. You can bring a hoagie and not be embarrassed to eat it. You can stand up and shout out the window if you want. Hell, you can howl at the moon if it makes you feel good! It's a B-FAB gathering. It's your time. No more thinking that you can't look good or find a great relationship, or that you can't work out and get in shape because of your ass. That's bullpucky. We're over it. There is nothing in the world your ass can prevent you from achieving and your B-FAB friends are there so you don't forget it! We say, "We're not going to take it any more! We only live once so we may as well live it as a B-FAB."

You Are Not Alone (aka the Cherry Pie Incident)

It's incredibly gratifying to be with a group of people who "get it" without long explanations. For example, it felt great to Janette one day when she told some fellow B-FABs the story of the only McDonald's cherry pie she ever had in her whole life. She was living in Philadelphia right after college and there was a subway strike so she had to walk back and forth from her job in Center City to her apartment in North Philadelphia. She walked by a McDonald's every day. This was in the days when they still deep-fried the pies. One day she broke down and bought a cherry pie, which she ate as she continued to walk home. It tasted great until that carload drove by yelling out the car window, "Fat cow! Give up the pie!" That pie was *way* less good after that.

Think how much better Janette felt when she met Joanie, who, upon hearing Janette's story, immediately confessed that she had had countless McDonald's fried pies but each and every one of them had been eaten sitting on the toilet locked inside a stall in the bathroom where no one could see her. Joanie felt vindicated hearing Janette's story. Someone might have said something horrible to her if she'd been caught eating pie, and Janette realized that McDonald's fried pies caused anguish for everybody, not just her. B-FABs in action. See what we mean?

You can come to www.EmbracingYourBigFatAss.com and share your pie story. Join our message board, where you can meet other B-FABs and be part of our first initiative: B-FABs Change the World. Let's form a coalition—a global movement of women coming together to celebrate stories of love and light and the pursuit of midnight snacks. We offer our confessionals in the hopes of someday hearing yours, thus shedding light on a normally dark and hidden place—your ass.

Come on. It will be fun. Janette will put her niece Beth Bee's unbelievable peanut butter cookie recipe on the website. Laura will blog about her daily trips to the health-food store. You'll meet people. You'll laugh hysterically. How can you lose? B-FABs come on board and B-Fabulous!

SECTION II

Your Life as a

Basket Case

Your Family, A Heavy Matter

ackling the subject of the family unit is at best a slippery slope, it's a complex, multilayered hodgepodge of life experiences that leads most of us to drink. This is not to suggest that everybody's childhood and early adult experiences were 100 percent horrible, but if you grew up with food issues of any kind, you were more than likely to be an emotional wreck 99 percent of the time. A young B-FAB's poor self-image is rooted in her funky family life and is a really crappy thing to contend with. Then you've got today's added pressure of anorexia/bulimia in young girls which has in no way been helped by the fashion industry's systemic obsession with the waif look. A great quote from Pat Benatar says it best: "Hell is for children." Bulging body parts can wreak havoc on a girl's life. They can often lead to the creation of her very own "I Hate

My Ass Club." Of course, some children were happy. (Janette and Laura could not be put in this category.) If you were someone who had a kick-ass childhood, if you were a true free spirit, then you're stuffed with fond memories. That's fine. We'll like you anyway.

Understanding what happened to you as a child takes a great deal of work. We're not going to do that here. Aren't you glad? We are. We're quite pleased that you bought this book and let's face it, humor books are a lot cheaper than therapy. Our mission is simple. We hope these words give you renewed power and ongoing success in blaming your parents for every problem you have today, especially those extra few pounds. If you need support digging up continued wretched memories of your past, join our B-FAB Society. We'd be happy to help.

Sitting on Old Family Patterns

Let's face it, your parents birthed you. You got their genes, their facial expressions, and often their eating habits. For most of us that's a fairly scary thought. What was it like at your dinner table? Did siblings or friends make fun of your girth? Were you the fat one of the family? The bottom line—family is family and they will all drive you nuts. You can never leave your past behind you. It follows you around from state to state and through some border crossings with all of it inevitably collecting on your ass.

Some of us can never lose weight, because of our terrible ancestral roots. At least that's what the scientists say. We kid you not. Our genes can be partially responsible for making us fat. That's the bad news. The good news is you can stop trying to look like Vanessa Williams in this lifetime. Sure, you could go back on the pineapple juice diet, hire a Hollywood personal trainer, and limit yourself to six hundred calories a day, but the minute you eat a real pineapple you are going to blow right back up. So go ahead and shake that family tree of yours. If you are fat, there's a good chance some other fat nuts are going to fall out. Oversized mothers, grandmothers, aunts, uncles, and cousins have all made you fat and it has nothing to do with whether they were nice people or not. Maybe they fought in the American Revolution, freed slaves during the Civil War, or invented the toilet plunger. It doesn't matter their heroic deeds: they made you fat. Be mad at them. Change your last name. Stop putting all that work into your family tree—its roots are swollen with yellow, glistening fat.

The Best Friend's Kitchen

Many of us spent endless days and nights at sleepovers at our friends' houses, especially if we preferred their mothers' cooking. B-FAB Laura's BFF (Best Friend Forever) growing up in Kansas was a girl named Sue. Sue's mom was a tireless kitchen person. They'd all hang out in this midwestern kitchen with the little window overlooking the perfectly manicured backyard while she cooked. Sue's mom would always be washing dishes, drying dishes, putting dishes away, then putting them back into a cooking pan to make more meals, use new dishes she had to clean up, then put away, and so on, and so on, and so on.

Sue's mom was a very nervous kitchen mother. She only seemed to be able to relax while cooking or cleaning, always on the edge of an emotional meltdown about something minor like her marriage not working or her teenage children having sex at a way-too-early age. Whatever. She took her angst out on the plates. She would scrub them until they were flat. Okay, dishes are already flat but she scrubbed them so much, so hard, so manically, well, if dishes weren't already flat, they sure would have been when she was done with them.

Laura preferred this touchy environment over her own home because her mom was not much of a kitchen mom at all. Sue's place always smelled of pies, macaroni, muffins, or home-baked chocolate chip cookies. Their best-friend camaraderie reached unparalleled heights in this cozy enclave with its small table and checkerboard tablecloth, tiny kitchen lamp, and kitchen phone for easy access to boy-calls. No matter what time it was, it was almost always time to eat. One of their favorite snacks was french fries loaded with catsup; mounds of steaming, salty fries fresh from the oven would be devoured in one sitting. There was a tremendous power rush found in this ritual of mixing raging teenage hormones with massive amounts of salt and sugar. This led to some fantastically wicked laugh attacks, which they used to call "spaz" attacks, saying over and over, "God, you are such a spaz!" We weren't worried about how many calories there were in a mountain of fries. To eat back then . . . was to play. The size of our asses hadn't totally crawled into our brains yet to ruin everything. These days Laura can't eat much of anything without paying for it later on the scale. Such a shame. But when she's out eating with her friends in nice restaurants, occasionally she can rediscover that place of female food sharing where everything is safe and yummy with laughter and fun. Thank God for food, friends, and a best girlfriend's kitchen growing up.

You Can't Hit a Moving Target

Laura has never been able to fully replace the comfort she found in Sue's kitchen. It is of course no wonder that to this day, B-FAB Laura does three things: 1) eats for comfort; 2) talks and eats with girlfriends for comfort; 3) is often gaining weight because she's an uncomfortable person. Somehow Laura has convinced herself that if only she could find the right house or apartment with that perfect kitchen, she could find that playful state again and stop worrying about her body type. It's not working. She's moved nine times in twelve years—for real. (Obviously, this lack of inner peace is not about where she's living, but don't try to tell Laura that. Right now her bags are probably already packed for her next home. It's a terrific weight loss program—she stresses out over the move, then has to lift heavy boxes and luggage over to her new temporary housing.)

Family Food Grabbing

Our eating habits and self-esteem issues that hold us captive were primarily formed in our own home, not our friend's house. So after a fun sleepover, B-FAB Laura would return home to her own family kitchen table facing the patio on West Seventy-fifth Street in Prairie Village, Kansas. Food was not so easy to come by there, only because her two brothers were such *fast* eaters! There was no chewing with them, only the "inhaling" of food. Laura had to be positioned, with fork lifted, ready to leap on that first helping, or she was going to be left out, just watching them eat. Her mom would make the usual: spaghetti and meatballs, pork chops or burgers. When her mother was ready to serve the food, Laura would start to get nervous because she knew that once it was on the dinner table, there would be a mad Banks dash, a survival of the fattest of sorts. Dinner was always on fast-forward with arms flashing, biscuits flying, and ladles of pasta being poured in midair barely making it to the plate, and then, *boom!* Dinner was over. Laura and her mother were left to load the dishwasher. Big Fat Coping Strategy: Arrive at the table ten minutes earlier than everyone else, before your siblings come in from a rousing game of baseball in the backyard, and nibble at the prepared food while acting like you're helping to set the table. You will be full before dinner even starts.

Competitive Family Eating

Every family dynamic is different, each as fattening as the other. Having siblings always creates the importance of learning how to be really good at putting dibs on food really, really fast. Maybe *you* were the fast eater of your family, which is a terrific tactic. You needed to eat your own food on your plate really fast, then reach over and pick off your siblings' plates, never missing a beat, and annoying the crap out of them. A classic line is to say "Are you going to eat that?" while shyly pointing at their plate. That's a good way to lose a finger. Brothers and sisters will scream at you, *"I hate this family. Get away from me!"* Fun for everyone! All the while, mother is demanding, "Eat your vegetables!" The problem is that we ate our vegetables along with everything else. (Maybe vegetables are fattening after all.)

Meat and Greet

To this day, Laura still has an issue with sharing food. If you have a chance to dine with her, which you probably won't because she doesn't know you, do not ask her to share her food with you. She'll think you're one of her brothers and slap you back so fast you won't know what hit you. If she chooses to offer you a bite of her vegetarian bologna, lettuce, and mayo on white bread, her fingers will be firmly positioned to allow your bite to extend only so far into the sandwich. She doesn't care if you accidentally bite her fingers. She considers this good boundaries. Splitting Chinese food is fine, but there must be a clear line of demarcation drawn down the middle and then the food should be quickly divided and served to the respective parties. This process resembles the parting of the Red Sea or George Washington crossing the Delaware. One extra scoop off that family-style platter and you'll receive Laura's glare of death. She's not going to have her food taken from her, nor will she be rushed to eat and if it means never seeing you again, well, fine. At least she has her food. Does Laura possibly have boundary and control issues? That would be yes. Dividing food portions sometimes is the *only* thing Laura has control of in her life.

The Family Refrigerator

One theory we hold to be true is this: to make a woman less frigid, stick food in her Frigidaire. Laura's dad was the best grocery-shopping husband a wife could ever ask for. Her family fridge growing up was always packed, in fact bulging with food. Every week her father would arrive home with sacks of groceries that would be neatly put away. Food shopping day was the most glorious day of the week, the most functional aspect of the Banks household. They made a lot of noise in the kitchen—creating shopping lists, figuring out what was for dinner that night, what time to eat, etc. Alas, they didn't make the same noise in the bedroom. Groceries never did really make Laura's mother feel more amorous toward her father, but he kept on trying. It seemed there were always more groceries than love. Groceries actually became the love currency, the main way her dad could show affection. (To this day, if a man doesn't buy Laura groceries, she feels unloved. Laura kisses her boyfriend wildly if he so much as brings home a bunch of bananas.) Laura wishes he were more of a shopper like her father and could show his love by going to the store more often. Laura has to do it. Laura hates this. Janette's boyfriend, Barry, shops for her. Why can't Laura's boyfriend be more like Barry? (Fortunately he makes up for it by reading her poetry in bed . . .)

Ultimately, the whole food and family thing turns out to be about you and men and dating. Isn't it all about that anyway? Maybe you've forgotten one of your first formative experiences, the one where you attempted to pull apart a box of cookies that said "open here." It wouldn't open. You couldn't rip it apart. You subsequently developed a complex for the rest of your life of being attracted to unavailable and closed-off men. Blame it on the cookie box.

What Having Kids Does to Your Perfect Heinie

B-FABs Janette and Laura don't have kids, so they can't tell you with authority what dire effects the little suckers can have on a gal's stupendous appendage (yes, her butt). But we are not the kind of authors to leave any stone unturned when it comes to researching "The Ass," and so to help us connect with you, the reader, as we try to enlist you into self-acceptance, we went out and found a few Mo'Beefa's (Mothers with Big Beautiful Fat Asses) to give us the lowdown.

TESTIMONIAL

B-FAB Dana from Oklahoma

I've been big, and I've been bigger. I've been described as "chunky" and "fluffy" and "ample." No one has ever suggested that I was "slight" or "petite." When I was pregnant with my second child, I was still carrying the twenty-five pounds I had gained with my first pregnancy, which was five years before. For me, being pregnant has so many perks, my favorite of which is not having to suck in my stomach. I'm always very proud of my pregnant belly and my maternal glow and having an excuse to wear all elastic all the time.

In the eighth month of my second pregnancy, I was faced with the unwelcome challenge of finding something suitable to wear for a business function, so I headed to our little town's bastion of maternity fashion: JCPenney. With my five-year-old in tow, I took a few items from the well-known Tentmaker Maternity line into the busy dressing room area. As I heaved myself into and out of various colors and patterns of tent-canvas-and-tow-rope-esque creations, my child, Little Miss Chatty McTalkerson, posed the question, "Mama? Why are you so fat?"

All of a sudden, the dressing rooms became deafeningly quiet. "Yes. Well, darlin', you know that Mama's going to have a baby, and our new baby is growing in Mama's tummy, making it big and round. Isn't it a miracle, dumplin', how tiny babies grow inside mommies and make Mama's tummy so big?"

She thought for a minute and I thought I was safe but then she said, loud and clear, "I know that, Mama, but what's growin' in your *butt?*"

Oh, the silence. It was so . . . silent. I muttered something about nice girls not saying "butt," dressed quickly, and decided that I didn't need a new outfit so much after all.

Now I'm thirty-nine, I have four kids, and I'm still carrying the twenty-five pounds I gained during my first pregnancy. And I don't care. I'm big. I've been bigger. I'm chunky in spots and fluffy in others, but I'm kind and loyal and funny as hell. Me and my Big Fat Ass are happier than I ever thought we'd be!

TESTIMONIAL

B-FAB Michelle

I always thought I would be one of those pregnant women who positively glow, the kind you can't even tell is pregnant unless viewed from the front. Reality check set in at about three months—who even knew *ears* could look pregnant?? Strangers would approach me on the street and claim that I must be carrying a little girl (basketball = boy, watermelon = girl). I would reply that I didn't know for sure but that's what I thought, too. What else was I supposed to think with a watermelon in my stomach and another watermelon in my ass? Reality check two: it's a boy!

It was a somewhat humbling experience knowing that your ever-increasing BFA has a larger purpose, yet wanting to complain about it all the same. One absolutely key ingredient for me was my husband, who thankfully seemed to have grown blinders when it came to my BFA (could my ass itself have been blinding him??). Both on the way up the scale and on the way down, which admittedly stopped a few pounds north of the start, he always found a kind word to say about my appearance—"Your nails look great today, did you get a manicure?" Seriously, though, a supportive partner works wonders in helping you to embrace that BFA—a BFA is still just a BFA.

TESTIMONIAL

B-FAB Marie

"Tons a bunsa" was the nickname bestowed on me by my brothers and cruel uncles when I was in my young teens. So I went on an orange-eating kick. (I only ate food that was orange.) I got into what I felt was the ideal shape. I was always a tomboy, competitive with the boys or girls playing any sport I could. By the time I was eighteen, I had worked hard to have that perky 36-24-36 Marilyn Monroe–type figure. But alas, all good things must come to an end. After my first child was born, I was a mess. The body had gone to hell. The boobs were sagging, the stomach was deformed with stretch marks, and the ass, oh, that poor ass, it kept following me wherever I went. My doctor was so unfair. He told me that no matter how much I exercised I could never get my ass back. It has been a yo-yo life of dieting for me. My ass is still hanging in there. It has never left me. I don't think it ever will. More than I can say for my first husband.

The Annoying Little Voice
Inside Your Head

Why does it seem that everyone has a great-ass life but you? Here's the secret: You might actually have a fabulous life but repeated, buried, negative thoughts in your brain are keeping you from enjoying it. You constantly hear that Annoying Little Voice (ALV) inside your head saying over and over, "If only I could lose that last 5–10–200 pounds I'd be completely happy and all my problems would dissolve." Nobody until now—not family, friends, church, nor the president of the United States—has really been helping us with this self-loathing thing we all have with our asses. You may feel that this is just the way it's got to be. Well, it's not. You just have to shut up your head.

Let's face it. None of us are fat because we're fat. We're fat because of something that came first. Genetics or emotions.

That's our view. Doesn't it sound professional and as if we really knew something?! What you think of yourself is what the world will think of you. You have the power to control your thoughts and, by extension, your ass. That Annoying, Ratty Little Voice might be in control of your life right now, but you can stop that. Replace that ALV with your own positive thoughts. This chapter deals with all the many ways you can tell your ALV to go shove it.

How to Stop Making Yourself More Miserable than Necessary

One way is to distract yourself from your constant derogatory thinking—the voice inside your head, the one that drones on and on about how you're not good enough, smart enough, or deserving enough. You know the one—you hear it so often you're used to it. You might not even care anymore. You might be thinking, So what. It's just inside my head. Inside your head is the *worst* place it could possibly be! (Have you forgotten about Joan of Arc?) We want to promote the end of the ALV. Your Annoying Little Voice spends way too much time ragging on and on about the layers of cellulite wrapped around your ass or insinuating that your new haircut is making you look enormous. Your ALV makes you sit on the sidelines at parties—if you go at all. Your ALV makes you nervous to ask for help at the mall or to stand up for yourself at work. There are many ways to silence this reprehensible, self-sabotaging voice. One great way is to simply sing "Three Blind Mice" over and over to keep your head full until you have something nice to say about yourself. (That sounds like we're making it up, but B-FAB

Janette has been using the "Three Blind Mice" redirect technique for years. Works like a charm. Far better than all that negativity.)

Eating Your Way out of Your Head

The greatest minds who have ever lived have told us that the Law of Distraction is the most powerful law in the universe. (We don't know who these great minds are, but they probably live in a university town somewhere, like Edinburgh. Or Oz. We're not sure.) Of course, the most powerful distraction of all is eating. Some were born to be food critics and make a living that way. Others invented TV shows, like Rachael Ray and Martha Stewart, but most of us don't make a living eating—we just live to eat. There is no activity that will shut up that Annoying Little Voice faster than a bowl of gravy with a side of mashed potatoes. Cold cereal is also good. Ideally something with oat clusters like Honey Bunches of Oats. Or granola. Five or six bowls and you'll forget whatever it was that was bothering you, for the entire time you are chewing. That's it, unfortunately: it only shuts off the ALV while you are actually eating. As soon as you can eat no more and your blue jeans have turned into a tourniquet, you start hating yourself for what you just ate. But yes, you have successfully completely forgotten about whatever it was you were eating to avoid in the first place. Wow. Who says compulsive eating doesn't work?

If you have the habit of eating while you watch TV, the best trick is to find something else to do with your hands. We can recommend knitting, crosswords, macramé, worry balls, handcuffs, or installing your own pillory. There are lots of easy ways to avoid food. Have someone lock you underneath the stairs like Harry Potter. That's a good idea.

An Overburdened Life

Here's a great lifestyle change that can shut up your ALV: Take on way too many responsibilities in your life. Put in fifty to sixty hours at the office, have four kids and sleep with your BlackBerry—ringer on. Become a true workaholic. There will be no downtime to let your Annoying Little Voice crawl into your brain patterns. You can be so exhausted all the time that at the end of the day, by the time you finish that last errand and midnight snack, your head hits the pillow and at that exact same moment, you pass out. Busy, busy, busy. Too busy to think about how you wish you were prettier, thinner, younger, or just about anythinger. If you choose the path of workaholism, we suggest you make it a point to save thirteen seconds a day for yourself. In those thirteen seconds, don't let your ALV start blabbing. Instead, embrace your BFA and realize how gorgeous and wonderful you are—then get back to working like a beaver. You might find that eventually you will learn to control that wretched ALV and stop working so darn hard, although we doubt it.

How 'Bout This?

Even if eating while watching television is the classic way to be at peace with ourselves, i.e., to turn off the noise inside our heads, there are other ways. You just have to get completely lost in whatever it is when you're doing it. What is that one thing you've done in your life, about which you can say that when you were doing it you liked yourself a whole bunch, deep down? For B-FAB Laura it's travel, writing, going to concerts, taking naps, and medication. Janette's head quiets down when she reads, when she gardens, and when she shoots clay pigeons. We suggest you find your passions. Live on the edge—take chances. Do what you want to do.

Your Ass Is Just the Way It Is

The Natural Laws of the Universe are random and cruel. Gravity sucks. Or maybe it's your genetic makeup that gave you numbers you don't like on your lotto-ball backside. Whatever it is that started this miserable ALV inside your head, you are the one that has to turn down the volume, darn it. Sometimes it seems impossible but it's not. We can send astronauts to the moon, and have them land with precision, so surely you can stop your negative thoughts about your own moon.

The Local Fix

LB: Co-Founding Member Confessional

 must confess: I love my local pharmacy. It's part of my personality. I like places that cater to my compulsive tendencies. It's at the local convenience store where I've packed it on, buying lots and lots of high-calorie snacks in jumbo sizes. Drugstores, too, allow for fast and easy purchases and a clean getaway. I love wandering around the aisles buying Pringles, Planters peanuts, M&M's, Ambien (show note from doctor), Nexium (show note from doctor), and Xanax (show note from another doctor).

When it comes to treats, most of them contain salt. If salt were an illegal drug I'd be incarcerated by now. I'm a lame drinker and not so great with sugar, but I can belt back a vat of salt like a blowfish. Second to salt, my drug of choice is . . . drugs. Not illegal drugs. Legal ones you can get from a doctor. I'm not sure which came first: my sense of anxiety and mild depression with a touch of sleep disorder, or the discovery of the drugs that treat them. Does my anxiety stem from being overweight? Probably. I can't imagine my compulsive behavior with food is *good* for nervous energy. My high-stress, burnt-out behavior probably relates directly to occasional binge eating of bad foods. Good. Now I can blame CVS for my ass. I do know I like to blame others for all my problems and I realize that's wrong. But I'm not going to stop blaming anybody. I'm just going to stop blaming myself for blaming others. (See the LB confessional "It's All My Mother's Fault.")

First I found Ambien. Wow, what a kick in the pants to get a good night's sleep for a change. Ambien is a perfect sleeping aid—until one day, it simply stops working. Then like a crack whore in search of a new street corner, I went on to the next pharmaceutical conversation with my shrink. He told me I could try combining Xanax with the Ambien. I thought, This has got to work. Ambien is for sleep. Xanax is for anxiety. Was I now going to sleep stress free? Does that mean there'd be no arguing in my dreams? I was convinced my doctor was turning me into Courtney Love, but all I wanted was a good night's sleep.

You might be reading this and thinking, Hey, I'm a B-FAB and I don't take drugs. Maybe your drug of choice is a gorgeous, moist mountain of strawberry shortcake or a Godiva chocolate martini? Maybe it's pointless sex with the neighbor down the hall or indulging in a pack of smokes. The point is, we all seek some kind of release from day-to-day stressors such as walking upright. (Living is easy. Easy living is hard.) I prefer pharmaceutical aids to chocolate. Some drugs accidentally increase your appetite. I heard one story about a B-FAB who took Ambien at

night before bedtime—in the morning there was a trail of chocolate from the kitchen to her bedroom to her mouth and all
over her pillow and face. This was a sign that the medication
was not working . . . nor was the chocolate. Sleeping and eating
at the same time is a sign that your body doesn't know what the
fudge is going on. This snacking-while-napping behavior is sort
of like somnambulism. Possible cures? Duct tape the fridge or
get a cat that attacks you at the first sign of movement.

A B-FAB's tendency to lose herself in all kinds of controlled
and uncontrollable substances is part of the pleasure of being a
B-FAB, isn't it? Do we have addictive personalities? Friggin' A
we do. Buying snacks and other chemically ridden products at
the local CVS gives me my quick fix, an easy checkout from
life's daily heartaches. I feel less alone munching on a bag of
potato chips, watching TV, and noticing that I'm almost kind
of happy for a second.

It's been a bumpy road to happiness, living as a B-FAB, a fine
dance in search of the perfect body-chemical cocktail that will
activate my pathetically dulled and salt-abused neurotransmit-
ter system. Happiness is fleeting and must be pursued with ven-
geance. Pain, on the other hand, can easily find you and last a
lifetime. The only hope for me now comes in the form of a very
low milligram of something to make me stop thinking about
whatever it is I can't stop thinking about.

So if I ever run into you at the local drugstore, just wave and
say hi to me. That would be nice. I'd feel more like I was part of
a collective. I would then have proof that the B-FAB movement has taken off. It's nice to make friends and who knows,
you may find me asking you, "May I borrow your discount card?
I left mine at home. I blame my mother."

Addictions and Compulsions
of a B-FLAB

(Big Flabby Ass Babe)

Being a perfectionist about your weight can really make you a threat to yourself, your pets, and others. Especially when you weigh yourself in the morning naked and tired, holding a cup of coffee. (Of course, it's good to set the coffee down before getting on the scale. The coffee cup alone could weigh a quarter of a pound.) When you get off that flat device from hell do you roll your eyes and give another long sigh because of the numbers you see? How could we have let ourselves go like this? Do you walk away disappointed because all you had was an apple for lunch the day before but the scale didn't move a digit? Do you then experience self-loathing for the rest of the day? (Self-loafing if you eat too much bread?) You have a problem with yourself. And hating yourself and your weight can force you to pick up a few nasty habits along the way. (For more on number phobias please see the LB confessional "Counter Intelligence.") In this chapter we are going to take a look at how your bad habits—the ones that don't make it on to your to-do list, can mess up your life. (For example, you don't write in your calendar, "Thursday, 5 PM, drink like a lush at the office party.")

On Top of Old Smokey

All the bad press in the world can't stop some of us B-FABs from smoking. Blame it on brilliant ad campaigns—a beige camel or a handsome, craggy-looking cowboy on a horse is all it takes to make you ready to light up. Why? We're addicts, that's why. Not to mention another big drawback: quitting smoking = overeating. Call it an oral fixation. Many a B-FAB who gave up her daily pack of Virginia Slims blew up like a balloon! Cigarettes start looking like a plausible alternative when you have to lay flat on the floor and pay a friend to help you zip up your pants. Some fat ass babes say, "To hell with it. I could give a hoot about a black-box warning. I'm a chain smoker. Shoot, you could get killed crossing the street! You can't live in fear." (We here at B-FAB Society Central do *not* condone smoking. We don't have to. It's already quite popular.) Add that first cup of coffee to a morning smoke and for some, there's no better cure to forget the size of your pants. The day's buzz has begun. Every part of you is energized, courageously prepared for what's next: wishing all day long that you were somebody else.

Another Fun Oral Fixation: Alcohol

Drinking is a wonderful device for going unconscious. For many of us there is just no way to accept the fact that we have nothing to look forward to—that how we feel in the morning (pretty miserable) is as good as we'll feel for the rest of the day. There's *got* to be a happy hour. So we start our meal with a couple of glasses of chardonnay (300 calories) and then we're able to forget about the calories in the rest of the meal (3,000 calories). Not only does it make you forget what you ate and your body type, you also forget your last name and the name of that guy that you're taking home tonight. What fun! Everything is fabulous after the first shooter. A great martini or highball can get any insecure B-FAB out of her chair and onto the dance floor shaking her enormous back forty. What a wondrous escape from our thighs—get hammered, weave 'n' bob around at your local watering hole, then go home and slip into a mild coma.

But wait: drinking hardens your arteries and makes you fat! Who cares? We're all going to die someday—even thin women. How is a B-FAB supposed to get through life without drinking? Some try to give it up and end up in Alcoholics Anonymous, eating brownies and smoking cigarettes in the back of the room. Most of us find a happy middle ground, indulging in the sauce long enough to have fun but still one step away from wearing a lampshade on our heads. Big Fat Tip: Do not drink and drive. If there is an accident, witnesses will find too many food wrappers stuffed into every crevice of your car.

Can't Beat Those Sugar Blues

While at the bar administering to our addictions, we B-FABs tend to enjoy the more exotic, sophisticated (better-tasting loaded with sugar) mixed drinks like stingers, Sex on the Beach, or piña coladas. Then we get both the alcohol and sugar rush! Yippee! Sugar is the best substance for going unconscious. We don't crave sugar, we live for sugar. Sugar is the Antichrist. It's a cane product from hell. They don't call it devil's food cake for nothing. Diabetes, heart disease, and cancer are a few of the things that threaten us. Who cares? Shut up. What's for dessert?

We can sometimes trick ourselves into thinking we're dieting by eating sweets as a main course. We'll have a bowl of ice cream for dinner or maybe a banana split. (That's fruit!) We know this is bad for us. Lots of things are bad for us. For instance, we find boredom to be a very life-threatening illness, and there's nothing worse than going out for dinner and not ordering Death by Chocolate. After that, you may need a smoke.

All Stressed Up and No Place to Go

Drumroll, please. The number one thing that causes fat asses to be fat asses that feel as slow as molasses, is stress. Yes, my dear friends, you (or someone you know) may more than likely be a nervous, overworking, overeating, hyperventilating wreck. Stress shuts down your body's ability to metabolize food. All the same, we crave food to calm us down. We eat and we're still nervous. Being an oral bunch, we'll sometimes neurotically call our friends and chat. This is what we sound like: "Hi, it's Mandy. How are you? What are you doing? I'm fine. I may go out and grab a bite. I'm kinda stressed out. Did I tell you that I saw my mother for lunch? I wanted to go to the gym and work out. That helps sometimes, but I was too hungry so I came home, and now I'm going out again. No, I don't know where I'll go, but do you wanna meet up somewhere? Oh wait, I've got another call. I've got to send an e-mail and the kitty litter needs changing. Can I call you back?" We can go on and on like this, saying nothing of substance. Stress makes you hyper and when you're hyper you forget about your backside. It's a small price to pay to forget that large problem. We're in survival mode just spewing our neurotic, stressed-out brain waves . . . and that's how we love it. Our daily activities can reflect this same stressed-out insanity. We can do things all day long and get nothing done. How great is that?

TESTIMONIAL

B-FAB Sherrie

Huddled around the television in my flannel pajamas, I remember watching the beautiful young ladies, with their perfect bodies, parade down the runways in their bathing suits and wondering if I could ever be like that. I overheard my mom and dad talking: "Sherrie will always be kind of short and plump. On the other hand, her sister will always be tall, lean, and elegant. *She's* the Miss America type." I felt my eyes begin to sting. My stomach went in knots as I tried to fight the pain of believing they were right. I was already chubby. My parents, well intended, encouraged me to do sit-ups every night, but that just reinforced my negative self-image. My parents' comments echoed in my mind every time I looked in the mirror for years to come. At one point my weight gain had reached an all-time high, and size eighteen was tight. I was addicted to sweets and carbohydrates, didn't want to be seen in public or purchase new clothes, or to have any photographs taken of me.

After many painful years, and with genetics of obesity, hormones, and age working against me, I was determined to overcome my weight challenges once and for all. I found the solution to be something much different than expected—stress management through supplementation. I also started drinking "superfood" protein shakes with stress-reducing ingredients. Now, as a mother of seven, and grandmother of five, I'm a size four. More importantly, I'm healthy, happy, and feel the best I've felt in my whole life! I believe that feeling beautiful is every woman's birthright.

Processed Foods and Other Chemicals on the Go

While out and about, we get food from KFC, McDonald's, Dunkin' Donuts, and other dens of debauchery, filled with chemically loaded delicacies. Often our metabolism is crap, from our bodies' attempts to assimilate all these saturated fats. Then we get irritable bowel syndrome (IBS). Sure, our bowels are irritable; you'd be irritable too if you had to deal with what's coming their way. Bloating is par for the course, the first course, second course, and of course, the third course. Acid reflux is nature's way of saying, "Stop eating now." It's an annoying interruption, often in the form of a belch or a burning gut. While at a romantic dinner, there's nothing that can turn off a date faster than having to pull out a jar of Tums from your evening bag. A B-FAB's digestive tract is working double time, leaving us constantly ready to pass out. Passing out is good. B-FABs would rather snooze than almost anything. It's best right after eating. We live to nap. Sleep. Pass out. Take advantage of your constant exhaustion, order another pizza, and ask for home delivery.

Meet Me Standing in Line at Starbucks

Here's another fun addiction—caffeine. Local coffeehouses are great places to get out of your head and into somebody else's. Catch a buzz and sit down on an oversized chair, if one is available, and talk mindlessly to a stranger. Order the really large, truckload size of java—you can live off it for the day. Sometimes people will drink coffee instead of eating. Even if it doesn't work and you still eat real food you will feel better about yourself because of all the cool, greyhound-thin actresses in Hollywood who are always photographed carrying a cup of Starbucks coffee. It's their way of telling the world, "We are drinking coffee and we are choosing this over eating and that's what makes us photogenic." It's easy to feel like a part of the in crowd while standing in some insane line waiting to pay inflated prices for coffee. You can do errands in your mind while you stand in line. You finally get to the front of the line, get your signature brew, belt it back, and you're good to go—jacked up at least until noon. Then you "spike" and come crashing down with the whole day left in front of you. Then you start again: "It's eight PM. I need another cup of coffee." Then you're up all night staring at your cat and hating your ass. The cat loves it. He has someone to play with in the middle of the night. B-FABs say, "Big friggin' deal that coffee dehydrates us and robs our body's natural ability to energize. We need our morning pick-me-up!"

But Don't Make Us Give It Up

We love our friends and family but whatever you do, do not try to save us. We don't like interventions. We're like whales. We need to learn to save ourselves. If we can't, good night and good luck. It's been swell, and what the hell, can somebody pass us the cream cheese? Mae West said it best: "I generally avoid temptation, unless I can't resist it."

To actually start to feel better from these ailments we'd have to give up sugar, salt, dairy, sugar substitutes, tea, soda, and coffee. Most would say, "Are you insane?" What's amazing is that while writing this book, B-FAB Laura has done exactly that and lost sixteen pounds in the process. She didn't do it to lose weight (that would not have been a good marketing strategy for this book). She did it to feel better. She made the choice on her own. Laura says, "Consciousness sucks . . . but it's the only game in town."

Checking Out

LB: Co-Founding Member Confessional

ecently my father bought me a membership to Costco's discount club. When your parents buy you things you have to accept them. I thanked him and marched over to the store to pick up my card. But did I really need to belong to this club? A company that prides itself on selling oversized amounts of food at discount prices? What will become of me?

I went to the membership desk and stood on a mark on the floor while they flashed a box camera in my face. I was happy that the shot wasn't full length. ID photos are never full length but can you imagine a club card with a picture of your ass for easy reference? Then, at the checkout, you'd have to turn around so they could match your membership to your backside. Actually, when they handed me my card I would have preferred a Polaroid of my derrière. I recall thinking that I looked like a bulldog with scurvy. That ten pounds the camera added, on top of that twenty pounds I'd managed to accumulate over the winter, amounted to an alarming photographic experience. The scowl that made me look like an inmate came from a place deep inside me where I hate what I look like. So when I saw that shot, I went there. The little voice sent me there. I couldn't help it. Why do I resemble a woodchuck? Why am I overweight? I know why: I overeat. Did I forget to go to the gym again? How much did I have to eat yesterday? Last week? Sometimes I can forget the fact that I'm heavy until I catch a glimpse of myself in someone's digital camera—usually at a party where a dear friend captured me with a cracker lathered in French onion dip dribbling down my mouth. "Say cheeeese."

I remember that critical voice in me saying, "If I'm this heavy walking into Costco today, how much will I weigh when I come back to renew my membership in a year?" Will the discount savings on crab cakes be worth the surcharge left on my waistline? I was very concerned. It all seemed so surreal. I put my new painfully honest photo of myself into my wallet, turned around, and entered the store. I was uptight about gaining weight just by walking in, imagining myself in one year on the *Dr. Phil* show via remote hookup, unable to get out of bed.

I had to ask myself, "Does a big store equal a big ass?" (Here is another reason why I have a weight problem: huge stores like Costco with no end in sight scare me to death.) I started to feel overwhelmed, stressed out, and confused. My breathing became shallow. I slowly resigned myself to my fears and started walking in with the other members, like a giant cattle call. (Mooooo.) The store went on into the next zip code. Hmm, maybe I could burn a few calories while shopping. Next time, I promised my-self, I'll wear my sneakers and work up a sweat while scoping the tofu mini-weenies.

I started out in the giant plasma screen section, and it was there that it started to hit me. I felt lost in a sea of flat-screen televisions, tube socks, lawn equipment, and frozen lasagna. Something was wrong—I could purchase four-layer guacamole dip next to lawn chairs, hacksaws, and gardening fertilizer. (This is a sign, my fellow B-FABs, that we may all be headed toward the end of civilization as we know it.) My only solace was found in grabbing recognizable labels with promises of low prices. I put a chilled Birds Eye eggplant Parmesan into my cart. It seemed intelligent because it was so much for so little money and eggplant is . . . low calorie. The only problem was that it was made to serve twelve people. Now I had to go find eleven other people to share it with.

I looked at my fellow shoppers. They looked like I felt—dazed and confused. I wanted to reach out and touch someone. Costco felt soulless with very few employees, and row upon row of glut-tonous proportions of food for sale. This is perfect for a culture based on immediate gratification. We are the Big Fat Gimme Generation. I felt ashamed of me and the club I found myself in and how easily I threw massive bags of food into my cart. Half the world is starving, but I can leave this store with over one hundred pounds of grub in my car, which grub will shortly there-after end up on my hips and thighs. I would confess to believing that . . . well, I'm just going to say it. *We are an overspending, overeating bunch of B-FABs, born in a wasteland of increasing waist-lines, with no control over ourselves or our backsides.* Places like this only fuel the fantasy that we can have anything anytime we want it. You have heartburn from the enchilada sample you tasted on aisle four? No worry, Pepto Bismol is in aisle 202. That's the club I'm really in.

At the end of this completely humiliating experience I ended up at the checkout line. Everyone is loaded up with jumbo-sized, nonrelated items, waiting for upwards of half an hour to get out of the club. (They don't call it a checkout line at this place by accident. You need to check out of life as you know it to stand there senselessly for what seems like forever.) I think it's Dante's third ring of hell. I think the valuable time you lose standing in line is time you could have spent on a job somewhere actually making money to shop in a more normal place. Everyone is standing around staring at one another's palletload of stuff, seeing if anyone else bought the breakfast bars and hair dye kit. Finally, you find yourself in the front of the line and it's your turn to check out. You quickly have to come out of your Costco coma to get your stuff onto the conveyor belt, get out your membership card with that original photo on it, and then quickly box all your stuff yourself.

By the time I'm pushing my massive cart out of the club I'm often a nervous wreck about how much money I just spent at my discount shopping membership place. (Once I purchased a twenty-pound bag of small appetizer quiches, soda, a sack of breath mints, and a massage table. The bill came to $295.00! I am not kidding you.) This is another reason I'm overweight. I'm broke. And when I'm broke the only thing that comforts me is eating. That's why I believe famous actresses are thin. Sure, if I were a movie star with $250 million in the bank I'd be happy, too. At least I'd look like I was happy, which is more important than actually being happy. At least that's what they say.

To get over the shock of my bill, I stopped and grabbed some nachos and a Mountain Dew from the little attached Costco food court. It was impossible to resist. There are huge glistening photos of hot dogs, bubbling sodas, and melting pizzas. (When I eat, I need to read something to take my mind off the fact that I'm eating. What I mean is I eat to go unconscious, but apparently I'm not unconscious enough, so I have to read simultaneously. I also need to read something while going to the bathroom. I guess you could say I've got myself covered going both ways.)

While snacking I picked up a flyer offering membership to the Costco Travel Club. I took the magazine home and read up on it at my place of business, the kitchen table. Then it hit me. Did I really want to vacation with my fellow club members? Did I want to look up from my lounge chair poolside at some resort in Orlando and see the guy I saw in the frozen food section? I'd yell out, "Hi, fellow Costco shopper. Remember me from aisle four? I bought the chips and dip and the box of Snapple. Hiiiiee!" (Waving wildly.)

Here is my confession: Dad, this year, I let my Costco club membership card expire. I love you. Thanks, but no thanks. Instead, I've got this little thingy on my key chain that I scan at my local A&P to get sale pricing. That's as close to a shopping club as I really ever want to get.

Romance and
Your Big Fat Ass

Romantic Moods and Moves

ome of us take a long time to hook up. B-FAB Laura feels like it's taken her twenty years to get it right with Daniel, her man of four years. B-FAB Janette didn't meet her longtime, wonderful boyfriend Barry until she was forty-two. That practically makes us experts. So if you find yourself still falling for losers all the time, you may need what we lovingly like to call a checkup from the neck up. Why do you keep falling for guys that act attracted to you in the beginning, then dump you like a hot rock after a few dates or a roll in the hay? Does your backside have anything to do with it? Of course it does. That negative self-assessment has been impressed upon you by your friends, your mother, TV, magazines, your mother, your coworkers, by society in general, and by your mother. Maybe your first boyfriend left you for the prom queen who had a tighter, firmer behind. Whatever happened or was said, you've picked it up and used it as a weapon against yourself. Your negative thoughts may very well be the reason you haven't found your knight in shining armor. What prince would want to be with Ms. Grumphead? If you don't think you deserve to be happy, then why should someone be drawn to spending his life with you?

When it comes to men, B-FABs can find themselves settling for second best. (This is explained in more complex, gruesome detail in the LB confessional "The D-List Boyfriend" and in the JB confessional "That Asshole, Todd.") The nasty name some men call women with fat asses is "easy target," but we say, "Bullhunky." You may be easier to find but that doesn't mean you need to fall for a guy just because he's showing you a little attention. First you have to find out if he's good enough for you.

So let the dance begin between the man and the B-FAB. Each testing the other to see what they can get away with, feeling for psychological loopholes, pressing ever forward, and looking for a connection. B-FABs beware. Take note of every tiny detail. Does he look in your eyes when he's talking to you or is he addressing your breasts? Is he looking at you as if you were a baby-making machine and interviewing your uterus? Make sure he's not constantly scoping the room for other babes. Does he make subtle remarks *of any kind* about your weight? Does he come back from the bathroom with a line of white powder under his nose? These are all signs that you have, once again, for a little attention, accepted a date with Mr. Wrong. (Mr. Wrong on the other hand could be a very nice guy. He would probably be Chinese.)

Rules for B-FAB Dating

1. Love yourself exactly the way you are.

2. Love anyone who is willing to love you exactly the way you are (within reason).

3. Find a man who likes to cook.

Growing Up B-FAB

B-FABs in high school were basically left out. We were the last ones asked to dance, to make out, to go anywhere or do anything with our dream date or, in fact, with anyone. It's a horrible thing—sticking out as the person no one would ask out because of either our own self-loathing or because of what we looked like. B-FAB Laura was so tall that none of the boys had a clue what to do with her. Laura's excessive height, not to mention the shame of her dysfunctional family, left her feeling like the Attack of the Giant Women. (Embracing your Big Fat Ass can be anything you are ashamed of, remember?) Laura didn't even expect to get asked to go to the prom, and she didn't. She went with her other tall girlfriend, Sue, and they just hung around the overly decorated gym feeling miserable about themselves. It's bad when boys don't notice you, as if you weren't even alive. It's so hard not to be jealous of other perfect girls who fit so well into the arms of their dates when they danced. How can you be with a boy when you don't fit with a boy, when you're bigger than he is?

The Battle of the Bulge

Yes, these days the world has indeed gone crazy with women wishing they were a size six. Many men today have also been groomed by the media to mainly appreciate a miniature backside. (Many, but by no means all.) We've decided to hate all the advertising agencies and all the stupid people in all those stupid boardrooms everywhere for deciding that we don't count because we're not all the Olsen twins! All the emaciated models on runways and in magazines, all the TV stars, the movie stars—they are all skinnier than a stick! This has imposed a mighty weight on us mere mortals. It has given us the urge to hide our asses in public, especially around men we're attracted to.

Make Peace with Your Piece

One of the best ways not to have your ass become the gravity-sucking-center-point-of-attention in public is to call a time-out between you and your backside before you even go on that date. Silence that annoying little voice inside your head by saying, "I don't want to hear one peep out of you tonight until we get home and I'm alone eating ice cream." Give yourself a pep talk before going out on that blind date. Talk to your ass: "My sweet ass, you and I are going to have a lovely night. We're going to have fun. We are hot! Sexy. I love you and me both." Put these thoughts on Post-it notes all over the house in case you forget. Stick them on your mirror. Take them down when your date arrives, but save them in an envelope labeled "Fat Ass Pep Talk," and put them back up when you come home by yourself. (This is actually a good thing to do. You can reframe your brain this way. It's called neuro-linguistic programming.) Putting positive notes all over your house, your pets, and your neighbors is a great way to keep your spirits up. (We are kidding about your pets. We're serious about your neighbor.) This self-talk will make your ass appear more attractive to him because he can tell that you are not obsessed with it or upset about it. (And why should you be? If he's worth anything he'll know it's just more to love.)

The most important thing to remember if you are trepidatious about entering the deep end of the dating pool is this: You are in control. Yes, you are. Here's Janette's philosophy from when she was out there dating every man who was willing. She started by asking herself what she wanted in a man—what she *truly* wanted before all the less important stuff like looks or jobs or kinky hobbies. Her answer was that she wanted first and foremost a man who wanted her. She had wasted *far* too much of her life in unrequited crushes on misogynistic or gay men until she was ready to get it right. (She did get some good decorating tips.) This philosophy freed her. If she went on a date and the guy didn't call her again, it was far less upsetting because he didn't have the important characteristic on her what-do-you-want-in-a-man list. He failed to want her. That's a turnoff. Janette didn't blame herself or her ass. She just thought to herself, He's a dud. Let's move on to Mr. Next.

So let a man be obsessed with your ass if he wants to be. It's not your problem. Bottom line: you cannot be likable, funny, engaging, interesting, or even worthy of a second date, much less a relationship, if all you can think about the whole night is whether or not your ass falls within some socially acceptable dimension. Stop giving your ass so much power. Whenever you are pondering your poundage you are focusing on your ass. You have now invited your ass to the dinner table like a third person on the date. Do you want the maître d' to seat you like this: "Madame? Monsieur? Madame's Derrière? Party of three—your table is ready."

Leave It to Cleavage It's more than likely that if you are somewhat overweight one of your best assets is your spectacular bosoms. After all, you've been feeding them, too, and they've grown nice and plump. Show off those puppies. Use a little push-up action. You can also wear red blouses with plunging necklines. (Red clothing, especially red panties, has been proved by research to excite a man.) Wear plum colors—maroons and lipstick-red nighties to get your man lathered up. Hell, go ahead and paint your ass red. Once you let go of the judgment you'll be amazed at how much fun dating and finger painting can be.

The Singles Scene with a Fat Ass

There are many places to meet available men—weddings, bar mitzvahs, First Communion parties, engagement parties, and pie-eating contests. These are places where food is part of the festivities and your ass will fit in just fine. Sometimes women refuse to eat in front of men they might be trying to land, but we see it differently. Start as you mean to continue—carry cookies in your purse! Let him know what he's in for. He'll love you and your pastries. (You'll be the best woman he ever had, but the grocery bill is going to be high.) He might as well know from the beginning that he can go ahead and have his own vices—eating is yours.

The secret to catching one man is to meet dozens of them. If none of your friends is getting married, become a wedding crasher. Attend sporting events no matter how much you hate them. If you pretend to love sports, many men are willing to overlook the crop in the outfield. If you know sports statistics, they'll overlook your statistics. Shout out batting averages while nuzzling up to your new honey to make more points and maybe get a hot dog. Sporting events are all about shameless pig-out eating and men who go to sporting events are big ol' cows themselves. If he can overlook your thighs, which have enlarged over the years due to too many hot pretzels and Cokes, you can accept his beer gut. (You could be perfect for each other. Just take off some weight before the wedding photos if you must; then you can pack it back on as a couple.)

TESTIMONIAL

B-FAB Betty from NYC

I've had many successful fantasy boyfriend relationships over the years, each one of those guys more accepting of me than the one before. Here's how I met one of my favorites. One day I was Rollerblading down the large loop in Central Park. Lots of people are biking, Rollerblading, and strolling around. Toward the end of my rookie season on Rollerblades, I felt brave enough to attempt the entire six-mile loop including the "big" hill. Well, you know what happens next. I was doing pretty good, until I came down the "big" hill. It was a Saturday and quite busy, but as I gained speed coming down, I couldn't help but notice over to my right, this gorgeous shirtless guy jogging in the same direction. As I passed him from behind still gaining speed, I turned my upper body back to catch a glimpse of his face. I immediately lost my balance backwards and landed splat on my ass, sliding some twenty feet along the pavement. When I finally came to a stop, at his feet, I heard someone ask if I was okay and looked up to see the very concerned face of that gorgeous jogger who had caused my fall in the first place. I had never felt so embarrassed before, but realized that I never would have ever met him if it wasn't for falling on my ass. He took my phone number but never called. I kept expecting him to. He never did—he was my fantasy boyfriend for the next year. Fantasy boyfriends come in handy on long, lonely winter nights. I imagined myself in his arms—getting up in the morning and putting on our blades, and him admiring my big, beautiful, bruised ass from all sides.

Intimacy on the Internet

Online dating is something that can drive you completely insane, yet if you don't want to bother with your makeup and hair style, it's a great place to meet a man. The wonderful thing about online dating is that, due to the computer, you can have access to thousands and thousands of them. They're like fish. Of course many of them are weird, oddballs, little liars, but isn't that often true with men wherever you meet them? The key is not to get overly attached to anyone too soon and to plan to meet at least fifty men before you decide on a keeper. You can actually, for once in your life, feel in control around the dating scene!

What's the Catch of the Day?

Once you've caught the attention of an alive and available person, it's time to go out on a date. A good place we like to go is restaurants. That way, even if you end up not really liking the guy, there's still something in it for you: pasta. One key point is to make sure your date is hungry before you go out. In fact, a university study reported in the *British Journal of Psychology* proved that men who were hungry were more attracted to heavy women than men who were full. We are not making this up! Remember this tidbit: to land your man, starve him.

We have some skinny girlfriends who say that it's not fair when a man buys you dinner and then tries to make a move. B-FABs say no problem. In fact, we'd feel bad if they didn't at least try. We'd think it was because of our ass. We'd think he wasn't interested. Of course we know better than to fall for that old trick—the one that says that if he buys dinner then we have to sleep with him. We're too smart to get pushed into anything like that, and obviously we're also not that shallow. To fall for that we'd have to be one of those bony women obsessed with our looks, a woman who totally fell for the stereotype of catching a man by what she looks like, then taking his credit cards and going shopping. We don't want your plastic. We want dessert.

Once you are seated in a restaurant with nice appetizers and low lighting, hold his gaze with your big bedroom eyes for more than thirty seconds. They've actually statistically proved that if you hold the gaze of a man for more than twenty seconds, he can get turned on—although some will run in fear. Either way, you've distracted him from your ass. If you see his eyes starting to check you out top to bottom, sneeze. He'll be startled and have to say "Bless you." He'll have to get you a tissue, all the while wondering if he's now going to catch your cold. See how you've succeeded? He is *not* thinking about your ass at all.

Par for the Course

So far you've given him a taste of who you are, but you haven't allowed him to move on to the main course—you. What does he think of your ass? Did he notice? Is he embarrassed? Will he call you again? Will he try to buy it a drink? Fear and dread can take over a B-FAB's mind as she imagines getting to the place with this adorable new man where he might be getting a first look at her bare ass. (Please note that this poor slob hasn't said a word. All this misery and angst is being created by you. He just wants to do it. Just so you know.)

Janette was so terrified about this that her relationship with her boyfriend Barry might not have even gotten started had he not said just the right thing at just the right time on their third date. He was flirting with her. He said, for some reason, "I'm very visual. *Very.*" Janette froze even though she realized that he thought he was saying something good, but, when she heard that, inside she thought, "Another one bites the dust." She was sitting there wondering how to end the date early. She said something in response to the visual comment. Something like, "Well . . . umm . . . I lost a lot of weight . . . umm . . . where's the waiter . . . look at the time!" Barry looked her right in the eye and repeated, "I'm *very* visual." Then he added the magic words, "I love Botero." Botero, in case you don't know, is an artist who paints and sculpts gigantic people. After Barry told her that, the date got even better!

So you've had your first date. If, after all this, he seems nice enough and there are sparks in the chemistry department, you might find yourself at some point in the future running the bases with him. When and whether he gets to third base is up to you and your outfield. (We assume you did a background check on this guy and discovered that he's not a hit man for the mob.) We do recommend safety first. And always remember, in the words of B-FAB Joan Rivers, "My best birth control is to leave the lights on."

TESTIMONIAL

B-FAB Lisa

In 1992, when I was young, in love, and maybe a little stupid, I decided to get matching tattoos with my boyfriend. Fifteen years ago, though never really skinny especially by today's standards, I had a nice healthy shape so I chose my right buttock cheek as the canvas. Ah, youth! Antonio, saying he wanted our love to be known to the world, chose his upper back just to the right of his shoulder blade.

As life progressed Antonio and I were separated by time, fate, and oh yeah, his *wife*. I gained ten pounds a year for ten years straight and watched with great curiosity and horror as my tattoo changed from the beautiful head of a unicorn with flowing tresses and a red rose in its mane, to what looked like a Picasso version of Medusa! Now seven years after losing that hundred pounds my unicorn is back! Yippee! Only now it looks a bit like she's been rode hard and put away wet.

Moral of this story: If your boyfriend chooses some random mythical animal, saying it's a symbol of his love, but refuses to put your name on his body, he's *married*! And oh yeah, never get anything bigger than the size of a bumble bee tattooed on your Big Fat Ass!

That Asshole Todd

JB: Co-Founding Member Confessional

wonder how many other B-FAB women have found themselves going out with men not because they like them but because the guy was willing. That brings me to my dreadful ex-boyfriend, That Asshole Todd. I met him in Omaha, Nebraska, when I was a stand-up comic. He was the opening act and I was the headliner. The poor thing, although handsome, was the most boring human being on earth. Why I went out with him is more than I can understand even now. He, naturally, found himself to be utterly fascinating. He would talk about himself for hours and hours and hours on end without punctuation and without regard for how many times he'd told the same story.

One of his favorite stories was about how he was in the rodeo club in college and rode bulls. You'd think that would have to be an interesting story, but not in his hands. I remember, even in the beginning of the relationship, watching the clock as he talked and thinking, I can take it for one more hour.

To underscore my error in choosing him, I'll tell you that he was also cheap. I remember the first time I went to visit him in the Midwest. We were going out to meet his sister and some of his friends. He said he had to go to the bank drive-thru, which we did. He withdrew ten dollars. I remember thinking, Ten dollars?! What on earth could one even do with ten dollars? Certainly not pay his half of the bill. That Asshole Todd never paid his half. If he owed eight dollars before tax and tip, he would hand over five dollars and feel that he had done more than enough. How do you spell "cheap bastard"? What on earth was I thinking?

For most of the first year of the relationship he lived in Kansas City and I lived in New York City. Finally, in December, That Asshole Todd was going to move in with me. He was very excited about the timing since he was arriving on the 28th and kept saying in our phone calls, "We can do our Christmas presents then!" He said it like it was a big exciting opportunity. It was our first Christmas together so I hadn't been sure about presents but that comment locked him in. I immediately went into debt Christmas shopping for him.

He arrived but kept putting off exchanging Christmas presents because he "wasn't ready." Then three weeks later I mentioned that I would be home late because I wanted to go to the January sale at the Betsey Johnson store on Columbus Avenue. "Can I go with you?" was his reply, which seemed odd since he had never exhibited an interest in women's clothing before. But whatever . . . I said he could come along. At the store, I rummaged through the sale rack and pulled out a large jacket that had been marked down to a small price. That Asshole Todd immediately jumped on it and said he was going to buy it as my Christmas present. That was why he kept putting off the exchange—he wasn't ready because he hadn't bought me a damn thing. I wanted to say, "Why don't we just go home and I can sell you something out of my closet."

That Asshole Todd was a great lesson: stop going out with men just because they want you to. As it turns out, you really need to like the guy for the relationship to really be worth it. (Who knew?) The point is, we are Big Beautiful Fat Ass Babes and we deserve men who are interesting, gorgeous, and kind, and who live only to make us happy.

Your Backside in the Bedroom

This is the ultimate test of a possible new boyfriend: Does he stick around after he's seen you butt-nekked from behind? Is his new nickname for you "Damn, Girl!"? Does he screech in horror when you get up to go to the bathroom? If so, dump him. That's why we must be in control of when and where we reveal IT. Let's face it, even a thin ass isn't the most beautiful sight to behold. Your ass is neatly tucked away and out of sight. Asses, often lacking in firmness, are designed by our great creator (She-God) to be positioned behind us and under our back for a reason. Often any light at all on the lower cheeks casts a sheen that can be blinding and, when you're trying to get into a romantic mood, a view of your big, blinding, protruding butt can really put a damper on amour.

News flash: He doesn't care about your ass—or maybe he

likes it. You are the one in the tizzy. Do whatever you need to do to feel better. The man only wants one thing—a piece of it.

And Now, a Word About Lighting

If your restaurant dates were managed effectively, your guy has already started to imagine you devouring him in the bedroom the same way you devoured that pork chop. Once you are sure you can be safe with this guy, take him to your place. Now that you are attracted to him and have realized that he's not going to call you fat, you need to get that first kiss to see if it's for real. That's why you're not going to his place. There are too many out-of-control variables and B-FABs like to be in charge. Do whatever you need to do to feel better and to let yourself feel sexy. The first thing we suggest is to install dimmer switches throughout your house. When you first get to your humble abode, turn the dimmer down really low so you can barely see each other. Sit around in the dark—a fat ass feels much better in a barely lit room.

Here's what we propose: Invite your beau over to your house, and place track lights in a perfect position so they hit your gorgeous big blue eyes instead of your gorgeous big blue butt. Liquor him up pretty good and pretty fast. When you're drunk, any ass is a good ass. Once it's dark and he's snockered, it's pretty much clear sailing. Have candles burning everywhere especially in places where things could easily catch on fire, such as next to the curtains, near the sofa, or (best of all) by your hair. This forces your guest to spend less time wondering how any woman could have grown such a big fat ass and more time freaking out about whether or not he'll survive the night. The key is to keep him preoccupied so he won't spend time trying to figure out how in hell you could have let yourself go like that. Other great ways to distract that hottie you have unaccountably lured into your home include burning dinner, lighting your couch on fire, or creating your own flash flood by putting a gopher down the toilet. All good solutions.

Mood Music by Fat People

Let's suppose, for one big fat minute, that you've happened upon that one great, single guy left in your hometown and you are miraculously dating him. You've taken him home and have gotten your mind off your ass long enough to enjoy him. Remember, you are the seductress and everything is going to happen at your pace, if at all. The next step is to set up your iPod with matching cute speakers to shuffle and play slow, romantic songs. The importance of music in setting the tone for the evening cannot be overlooked—in the background play the music of heavyset singers and artists. (It will drown out that barking beagle in the alley next to your bedroom window.) While Mr. Next is listening to large, throaty singers wailing away, he'll be unconsciously getting in the mood for what you may be about to expose—your ass in two zip codes. Play Aretha Franklin, Ella Fitzgerald, or maybe the later years of Elvis Presley. Your man will be subconsciously thinking about hefty people and he'll be more accepting of you by comparison. Other artists in this lineup include that *American Idol* guy Ruben Stoddard, Big Daddy Kane, most opera singers, the later years of Linda Ronstadt, and the early years of Luther Vandross. (Do not put on any of the music of Snoop Dogg. He's just too damn thin.)

The father of making love in the dark is the master himself, Barry White. Everything about B.W. is about being okay with fat. His voice has that wonderful, throaty I-just-finished-a-sandwich quality to it. And the music is sooo slow. That's an important point. Slow music sets the pace so your lover doesn't expect you to get up off the couch too fast. When you're carrying excess baggage in your derrière, getting up from any seated position takes a fair amount of thought and preparation. Barry in the background keeps the whole night in slow-mo and we ladies know how important that slow-mo is to any successful roll in the hay. In other words, you're chunky for a reason. This should be a cue to your beloved that you want him to take his time loving and caressing, licking and kissing, until he practically passes out. Romance with a fat ass is not for the faint of heart. It takes stamina to keep up with us. Before a night of romance, we expect to eat more food, drink more alcohol, and we suggest short catnaps between each meal and makeout session.

Moving On to a Steady Relationship— New Options for Feeding Your Fat Ass

It's a great idea to snag a man who likes to cook and grocery shop for his gorgeous B-FAB. The ideal man should buy us all the things we like to eat and place them in the fridge lovingly displaying the labels of pretty bright packages. (Skeptics may claim no such man exists, but that's not true. BFA lesson: don't take the man you don't want because it might make you miss out on the one you do!) There's no greater aphrodisiac than seeing a grown man naked, holding nothing but a spatula or putting away canned goods. It has been statistically proved that it turns women on to see a man cooking and fussing in the kitchen.

It would be fun to keep your man barefoot and in the kitchen as much as you can. Grab his Palm Pilot and schedule in the following chores: Monday—go to the grocery store; Tuesday—prepare tasty dishes for the entire week and put them into handy little Tupperware containers; Wednesday—unload the dishwasher (B-FABs are much more likely to be in the mood if the dishes are done); Thursday—prepare us our weekly candlelit romantic dinner; Friday—make love to us while feeding us chocolate-covered strawberries. Saturday is a fluff day, so tell him to fluff up your lovely fat ass couch pillows so you can be more comfortable. Sunday you can love him to pieces and be his slave. Call him your hero all day long. Thank him so much for helping with the cooking and cleaning, with him wearing

Terrific Bathroom Trick When you are first dating it feels like you will never in your life want to say no to his advances. Once you've snagged and tagged him, though, things might change a little. So what do you do if he's in the mood on a given night and you're not? You can go into the bathroom and not come out for hours. Create all kinds of emulsions and rituals that keep you locked away for at least an hour and a half. We enjoy: face washing, pimple viewing, shampooing, bathing, hair brushing, flossing, water picking, nose picking, hair plucking, foot stone scrubbing, and just plain going to the bathroom, to name a few. By the time you come out, he will be asleep. You are then free to watch Letterman or snack on a lovely low-fat muffin or maybe some Oreos.

nothing but a French maid's apron or western chaps. Either one is a nice look. He should also be allowed to watch the game or the fight on TV on Sunday. If you really love him, you can pretend to like it, too. That, our B-FAB friends, is the secret of a happy cohabitation.

Wedding Vows for the BFA

If you decide to get married, choose a guy who will stay with you even if your ass gets larger. It very well may. Make him commit to your ass out loud in front of all your friends and family. Put it into the wedding vows. Have him look in your eyes and say, "I will love you through thick and thin—mostly thick, in fatness and in health, until death do our asses part." If he's willing to say those words (and if he's not checking out your maid of honor just a little too much) he's yours! Now go eat cake!

The important thing to remember is that he is marrying you, not your ass. There is no need to be jealous of skinny women. If he wanted a skinny woman he wouldn't have wanted you. You're safe. It's okay. You are beautiful and loving and wonderful. You deserve a great relationship. Nobody at your wedding cares at all about your ass except you, so just forgive yourself and have a nice day. Go forth.

TESTIMONIAL

B-FAB Rosemary

From the very first date until we finally got married, my ex and I had very little sex. When we did have sex it was bad sex. I stuck in there, hoping that with practice it would improve. I was in my early twenties so what the heck, I didn't know any better, so I let him take the lead. There were times, okay, actually once, that I had a good sexual experience with my husband. I finally had an affair. It was short-lived but it did the important thing of reinforcing the fact that I was okay with my sexuality.

I've always had a poor body image and my husband only reinforced my low self-esteem. If I had felt better about myself, I certainly would not have put up with all of this. After six years of marriage, this thing called est training appeared in the newspaper. (est stands for Erhard Seminars Training, which was a transformational seminar popular in the 1970s and early 1980s.) We both knew we needed some help so we enrolled. We took it together and during that time I got a better grip on myself. I came back from the seminar with a new approach. I had gained about ten pounds, eating over my frustration and stuffing my feelings.

I decided that I would lose some weight to try to be the way he wanted me to be, what he wanted to look at. But when I approached him for sex, he always would say, "You're a little too heavy for me to be attracted to you, honey." At that point I weighed 120 pounds at five feet four inches, which I thought should have been thin enough! But after that remark, I ate only lettuce for weeks. Suddenly I was 108. My friends thought I looked emaciated. One Saturday, I ran up to him and said, "Look I'm thin! We can have sex now." He looked at his watch, and said, "Right now I have to go to the hardware store, maybe later." I knew then that it was over.

Later that month, he asked me straight-faced, "Would you

consider it cheating if I wanted to sleep with a man? Wouldn't it be different than if I were having sex with a woman? It would be a kind of an . . . experiment." I said, "No." We broke up. Immediately after we broke up, he met another woman, asked for my engagement ring back (it was a family ring), gave it to her, got married, and got her pregnant right away. I knew he was proving to me and to himself that he was not gay. I got into therapy and joined Overeaters Anonymous, where at first they laughed at me for being too thin to be there. I went on to create a new life for myself. I used food to hide out, to not make the changes I should have made earlier to improve my life. It also created a new pathway for members who were not overweight but used food in a self-hurtful way.

The D-List Boyfriend

LB: Co-Founding Member Confessional

Why am I so unlucky in love? My latest theory is that since I never had that perfect figure, I never had that perfect guy. I never bothered with eating right or going to the gym so I always ended up with seemingly subpar boyfriends. I was the "runner-up date" because they couldn't get the girl with the flat stomach. I have no idea if this is true or not, but if there were truth in feelings then this would hold up with Judge Judy. In some of my past relationships, although not all of them, I felt like the default girlfriend. I was the D-List girl, dating the D-List guy. (An A-Lister is someone who I imagined was out of my league.)

What is an A-List boyfriend? Most of my life I've been obsessed about finding a superhero guy with all the right everything—funny, successful, and of course, handsome. He had to be movie-star gorgeous. If he had too much chest hair or his private parts were too small, I stood in judgment. (Small private parts for a man is our version of a fat ass, but at least men can hide their parts easier in their pants.) Isn't it hypocritical for me to judge a man on his looks or his reproductive organs and then have a hard time with him judging me? (Life is complicated, isn't it? I wish I weren't so shallow. I'm quite sincere when I tell you that it's all my mother's fault.)

Speaking of my mother, she raised me watching old black-and-white movies with all the great movie stars—Clark Gable, Cary Grant, and my mom's favorite, Leslie Howard. She wanted to be a movie star, which is why I became an actress. It's her fault I'm obsessed with looks in a man. I ended up starring in some films myself. (See the LB confessional, "Working for Food.") I had three very handsome leading men—and with all of them I experienced the celluloid bliss of an on-screen kiss. (Don't believe those actresses when they say that love scenes are not a turn-on.) I even produced a documentary film, *The Manhattan Dating Project*, which is all about finding true love and how it relates back to animals mating in the wild. How do they do it? By smell. So do humans. That's what is so difficult about Match.com. Maybe someday they'll invent the scratch-and-sniff computer screen.

Speaking of smell, here's a real stinker of a story from my dating years. This roller-coaster relationship epitomizes my desire for perfection in a man, and their desire for perfection in me, and in the end the whole deception falls apart. When I met Rich I was ready to fall in love—I immediately projected that desperate desire for attachment. I hadn't had a decent date in months, so I was set up to be knocked down like a bowling pin by any guy who looked good in a pair of jeans. I began online dating, which had turned into a living quarantine, a self-imposed asylum, hours and hours spent online looking at made-up profiles of men who didn't really exist. Fantasy boyfriends. Nor could I reveal my true stats online because nobody would ever ask me out! I couldn't reveal my actual age, my dress size. I wanted to be in the "athletic" category but I belonged in the "robust" group. I knew it was a waste of time. Men on Match .com always seemed to be looking for women half my age. (There seems to be a high demand for thin, submissive twenty-two-year-old females from Asia.) A friend said I should try JDate.com but I was Episcopalian and I knew most good Jewish boys don't end up marrying shiksas. I finally came to my senses, realizing that online dating had no connection to real life. It was just an extension of my imaginary boyfriend thing. I realized that, if I wanted to land a live one, I had to check into the land of the living.

I checked out a calendar of upcoming events. There was a film festival in Greenwich, Connecticut. The main event was at a Rolls-Royce and Mercedes-Benz showroom. This seemed like the perfect place to meet a man who had a love for film and the arts and could possibly buy me a Ferrari. The movie screening before the reception was packed so I was hopeful that there would be lots of men to choose from. Sure enough, the film ended and we all herded into this magnificent showroom, gleaming from end to end with giant, gorgeous cars, and giant, gorgeous men.

I beelined it straight to the buffet table. Oh my God, the food was great. I was making a mess of myself as I often do with some cheesey concoction and a dozen cocktail napkins when a man walked up with his friend, who introduced him. The man was tall, about six three with big shoulders, big blue eyes, big hands, and a brown suede jacket. He said hello, and smiled with the most perfect white teeth I had ever seen in my life. He took my phone number. I sensed he was just as desperate as I was to meet someone and that the phone would be ringing shortly. I've often thought they would call and they don't, but this one did the very next day! He pursued me for many months. He finally won my heart with true words of love, affection, connection, tenderness, and really nice dates in fancy restaurants.

The first three and a half months were great. Five-star restaurants in Greenwich were a big plus. One of the restaurants was so fancy that I ended up sitting right next to Diana Ross! We did lots and lots and lots of fine dining. Then it started to creep in . . . subtle remarks about my weight. He'd show up for a date: "Hey, did you put on a few pounds?" In hindsight, of course I'd put on a few pounds. He was taking me out to eat every night of the week, allowing me access to the most delicious, saucy duck entrées, steaks, and desserts. I should have screamed at Rich, "You're the one who's been taking me out to eat every friggin' night of the week! If you want me thinner take me ballroom dancing!"

I started packing on the pounds. He was right. By the third month I felt like a pig going to slaughter. Then he presented me with an irresistible offer. He wanted to take me to the Caribbean—to Saint Thomas and Saint John, where we'd stay at the Ritz-Carlton hotel! Now I felt like a boar that had been put on the rotisserie in the Caribbean heat. I went. I must say that the scenery was beautiful but there was a problem: at this point not only had Rich become a contemptible person, criticizing my appearance in my tight bathing suit, but now he was also hammered!

We flew home and by then it was February and the fine dining had turned my not-so-fine figure into a chunky, God-my-pants-hurt nightmare. Valentine's Day arrived. We did what all couples do and what Rich and I had done nightly since we met. We went out to eat. After dinner he presented me with diamond earrings. I had never gotten such an expensive gift so romantically presented. But I could sense an undercurrent and it wasn't just acid reflux. As I practically lifted the plate to lick off the last drops of some exquisite sauce, he was becoming his usual temperamental self on his fifth glass of wine.

As soon as we got home he broke up with me and stormed out of my apartment. He said, "I'm going home." I had never seen his apartment. (In retrospect, that's a sign.) The next day he called me on the phone. I couldn't actually see his blue eyes and his shiny white teeth, which may have made this easier to hear. "Laura, I don't love you. I have never gotten over my last relationship. You met her. She was in Frankie and Johnnie's Steakhouse, sitting at the bar. Well, I'm going back to her to try to work it out." (I did remember seeing her. She looked much thinner than me.) Then it got even weirder. He thought he had hung up the phone but he hadn't disconnected me and I heard him saying, "Yeah, I broke it off with Laura. That was going nowhere. I've wanted to break up with her for a long time. Yeah . . . I gave her the earrings, but I kept that one-carat diamond pendant. I'm giving that to my daughter." I didn't know which to be sadder about: him or the necklace. I think the necklace. If you could lose weight by crying, that night I would have lost a few extra pounds found around my thighs.

The lesson for any smart B-FAB is to enjoy a man who wants to wine and dine you. Say in advance, "If you put me in front of fancy food and elaborate sauces, I may put on a pound or two." If he doesn't flinch after that, go for it.

For those of you reading this who have no idea what I'm talking about, that means you are a normal B-FAB who probably had a really nice, normal mother and family. You had good role models and everything explained to you. I wish your mother had been my mother. I wish I could stop blaming my mother. I wish I could stop writing now. It's midnight. I'm going to bed.

Clothing, Friendship, Shopping, and Other Distractions

Fashion—Not Just for Skinny Babes

Janette loves clothes because she can express herself and hide behind them at the same time. She has a photographic memory and can tell you what she wore at every major event of her life. For example, the first time she headlined as a stand-up comic it was in Orlando, Florida, at a club called the CopaBanana. She was wearing a fairly large gray and white striped wrap skirt from Banana Republic and an orange sweater into which she had pinned enormous shoulder pads. Her thinking at the time was that if she didn't mind looking like a linebacker, she could definitely minimize her hips. At that point it didn't enter her head that she could be a size sixteen and actually look good. Now we know that you can look great at any size but when Janette was younger she was relying on the fashion strategy that you read about in every magazine, called the Art of Distraction. Wear a bright purple scarf and big hoop earrings and no one will notice the size of your ass. Our real problem with this is that the message is that a big ass can't be attractive to ourselves and others. Au contraire. Janette once knew a waitress with a well-fed BFA who didn't mind having it in the least. She used to wear these great skirts that hugged her hips and then fell loose around her legs. This B-FAB was really hot. She didn't try to *hide* her ass. She simply dressed it for success. Thanks to the magic of clothing, your ass can look great at any size. The first question, as you look in the fitting room mirror, shouldn't be "Does this make me look thin?" It should be "Does this make my ass look Latin—in that good Jennifer Lopez kind of way?"

The B-FAB Art of Distraction Why wear an alpaca sweater when the whole animal provides such better coverage? Get your own alpaca and be sure to have it always standing between you and anybody that might be looking at you. It is sometimes more convenient if you get yourself a whole herd of animals. Not only will no one notice your ass, you'll also make a great photo op for tourists so you should be able to get in lots of people's pictures. The final, added advantage is that, if anyone gets too close, alpacas tend to spit, making for great action shots.

What You See Is What You Get

Clothing exists to make humans feel less embarrassed about their bodies. Here's how it all began. Neanderthal man started losing his body hair . . . *and* he went bald. His wife was so horrified she threw him a goatskin and clothing was born. (Soon after, this gave B-FAB cave ladies the tip-off that they were butt-naked, too, only they needed clothing at twice the price.) Fast forward to the truth about you. The right outfit is as much about how you feel about yourself as it is about how you look. A B-FAB never conforms to a fashion trend. B-FABs don't do what designers tell us to do. We'll hide our bodies however we want to and choose what styles we love and what we're comfortable in.

Fashion is just a tool that can make you look and feel your best. Even on a day when you can't feel pretty by yourself, the right outfit can turn that around. It's hard to feel ugly wearing a Luna Luz skirt—the one that ties underneath to make billowy asymmetrical flounces with a soft, comfortable yet fitted cotton-spandex yoke at the waist. Throw on some capri leggings so your thighs don't squeak and you can walk around feeling gorgeous (as you are). The Luna Luz skirt size extra large fits up to about a size eighteen or twenty and would make anyone feel like a size six. All you need to add is a men's V-necked t-shirt (roll the sleeves up by two folds) and, if it's chilly, a long rectangular scarf that hangs down the front and you can go anywhere looking as good as anyone and feeling better than most. That's what fashion is all about.

You know how self-help books and seminars always tell you, "Act as if." That means, if you don't feel confident but act as if you *are* confident, you will become confident. Well . . . that stuff works. Clothing is a great place to start acting as if because it can make you feel however you want to feel, and how you feel affects how you act. If you are interviewing for a corporate job, for God's sake wear an elegant yet conservative suit. (Hide that wild woman!) *Clothing* is just another word for *costume*. Dress like an executive director, even if you don't have the bank account. You'll feel like a VIP (Very Impressive Person) and you'll walk into the interview more likely to get the job! On the other hand, walk in dressed as Annie Get Your Gun and, frankly, you deserve what you get. Basically in that situation if you didn't get the job it would be because of your six-gun, not because of your ass.

Colorful Comfortable Clothing

Just because something makes you look thin doesn't mean that you will walk around feeling great in it. For example, if it only works when you're looking in the mirror holding your breath, that's not a great B-FAB pick. You aren't all that attractive when you're blue and not breathing. Comfortable clothing helps you forget the actual size of your body and leaves plenty of room for pie. That doesn't mean you should, under any circumstances, go out and buy another black tent dress because someone has convinced you that black is the only color you should wear. That's crap. You can look as good in rainbow colors as anyone else. You'll look less depressed wearing yellows and blues and reds and greens. Sometimes it isn't easy for B-FABs to find the right comfortable and colorful ensemble. It's just the way it is. Don't give up. Chico's does better than most chain stores (although we could swear their sizes keep shrinking). And just to prove we B-FABs are becoming mainstream, Janette recently stopped into Target for the first time and was surprised to find some interesting and B-Fabulous designs by Isaac Mizrahi. She bought an adorable dress that was cut to give her a lovely waistline, but it was also pleated and lined and still loose enough to completely disguise her spare tire that pops up when she sits down. So, you see that if you look for them, the clothes are out there. That Target dress was thirty-five dollars (not on sale!) and it makes Janette feel younger and thinner. It's just a dress but she can pull it over her head and feel better all day and this for just thirty-five bucks. See. Clothing is important! Grab your B-FAB friends and go hunting. You don't need a shotgun or a permit . . . just patience, persistence, and a little bit of luck. A shopping spree with your B-FAB local can be an unbelievably uplifting experience!

A word of warning: Many of us have thin pretty friends. It's not their fault and we shouldn't hold their shortcomings against them, but we should also definitely *not* go shopping with them. You are unlikely to feel great sharing the fitting room with a size two. Be friends with anyone but shop alone or with another B-FAB.

Choosing Your Own Style

Friends and coworkers love to give Janette their opinions about her appearance on a regular basis. "You should wear tighter clothes," they say. "You're not that fat." She responds, "Key word *that*." They ignore her and press on. They insist. (What's their problem? Can't they be seen with an extra large?) They also try to get her to try on size twelves. At five three, Janette is a size sixteen on a good day—she's making the right choices.

She wears loose, flowing clothing in natural fibers and prefers fabric with weight to hide her weight. Her clothing then hangs from the shoulders or waist and doesn't get caught up on the lumps. (Lumps don't work in gravy, either.) The point here is not that you, the reader, are necessarily going to look best in looser clothes. The point is that you have to find stuff that's actually right for you and then you will feel comfortable and more confident whether what you've chosen is tailored or frilly-girl-laced. Good gravy, take the time to put together your outfit. It's okay if it takes a lot of time and fabric. It will be worth it in the end. (We don't mean death—we mean your ass.)

I'll See It When I Believe It

Janette has always loved clothes and craved a bottomless closet. To this day there is nothing she enjoys more than shopping. When she was growing up, nothing in the Chubbette department at Sears was quite as glamorous as the outfits she dreamed about, so she used to spend hours and hours sitting in a chair imagining herself thin and wearing incredible ensembles. The daydreams would also, of course, always have some shadowy handsome man who would be about to sweep her off her feet, but she didn't spend much time thinking about him. He was the ending. Mostly she thought about what she'd be wearing when she met this mythical "him." Sometimes she'd be stuck in the middle of a daydream just trying on outfits in her head because she couldn't decide what to wear. Should she choose a celery-green formal gown with an empire waist, flowered bodice, and flowing chiffon overskirt, or would the white low-waisted flapper-style dress like the one Liza Minnelli was wearing in *Cabaret* in the scene where Sally Bowles meets Maximilian be better? Every book she read, every catalog she saw or movie she watched gave her ideas for the kind of clothes she could wear one day—if only . . . if only she were thin.

In retrospect, she lost a lot of time dreaming about clothes when she could have been buying them. Here's what she wants to tell her fellow B-FABs: Don't wait. Waiting to do things until you get thin is a waste of perfectly good living time. Start now. Allow yourself to look and feel great exactly as you are and your weight will become whatever it's supposed to be. Stop wishing you look like Nicole Kidman and for God's sake go get in the car and go shopping—there's a two-for-one sale at Wal-Mart!)

Years passed. She became a stand-up comic and lost all her weight (see her confessional "My Life in Diets"). On her thirty-sixth birthday she ended up in San Francisco, thin and between gigs. She had just shot her first national commercial for Spic 'n Span laundry detergent and had the first credit card she'd ever owned. A size small meant only one thing—shopping. Gorgeous brown and black checked rayon palazzo pants and a black and white striped cashmere sweater. Floral print (size eight) suspender pants and a black cotton cropped Betsey Johnson sweater. By the end of that week she found herself in her hotel room with all these clothes to choose from to go on a date with a man she'd just met. He was a former Marine and Top Gun pilot. (He'd even flown some of the jets in the filming of the movie *Top Gun*.) But the more interesting thing was that she was getting ready for a date with a very exciting, glamorous man and she was trying on all the outfits she had bought in her week of I-just-did-a-commercial-so-I-don't-care-if-it's-not-on-sale shopping . . . just like in her years of daydreams. She had an epiphany. She was there in San Francisco that day with all those outfits, going on that date all because she had been imagining it her whole life. That was the moment when she understood that she really *had* thought herself thinner . . . and if she

could do that, she could do anything. (Right now she is working on leaping tall buildings in a single bound but it is taking
more practice than she expected.)

Shopping with Your Billowing Behind

The problem is that there are still too few designers of large-size
clothing. It's not impossible to find great outfits, but they tend
to be more expensive. You'll be more likely to find great styling
in smaller boutiques. B-FAB fashion tip: buy a few great quality
things in incredible fabrics, and then burn any double-knit
polyester tops or pants—take them off before you ignite.

Some women hate their bodies so they hate shopping. Every
time they try on something that doesn't fit, it makes them hate
themselves. Isn't that sad? Why blame ourselves when we
can blame the clothing companies? It's their fault for only making clothes that fit a broomstick. Our mantra: it's not us—it's
them!

Open Letter to the Fashion Industry Helloooo!!
What's the matter with you? Does the word Latifah mean nothing? How can you look at her, or at Mo'Nique or at Emme (that
gorgeous plus-sized model) and say you can't have a BFA and look
good? *Design* for us! No, we don't look good in double-knit polyester sweatpants with a tight top that does nothing except highlight
our cellulite. No, we don't look good in Paris Hilton pink. (And we
are not about to accessorize with a small chihuahua.) We are not
Britney Spears or even Hilary Duff. We are great Big Beautiful Fat

Ass Babes and we deserve clothes that make us look and feel great.

You tell us that our body types can't look good no matter what we do. On the other hand you still want us to spend our hard-earned money to buy clothes from you. All you do is take some golf shorts that would look good on Jessica Simpson and make them in a 2X and then we wonder why we don't feel good about ourselves!

Here's another thing, Big Fashion Designers: *All* your tops are too short! Shop in a normal place like Sears—every top you find ends just below the waist, making a nice horizontal line straight across the widest part of the body instead of continuing on to just below the thigh saddle bags so only the thin part of the legs would show. That is just cheap. Fork up the extra foot of fabric why dontcha?

Thank you for your attention, Fashion Industry. We think we can still be friends. We're just saying what we think. If you need help about how to make clothes that look good on B-FABs, call us. We have lots of ideas. Janette is dying to market her new "Hip Hider" idea. We'll do a B-FAB clothing line if we have to, so don't say we haven't warned you. Thank you and we really like you any-way. We really want you to like us, too. (We have to say that in case we have to work with you later.)

Haglike Annoying Harpies Who Interfere with Your Shopping Enjoyment

The next serious shopping issue we have to cover is that there are many stores that you simply have to avoid because the salespeople are so *annoyingly* helpful. That's also another drawback to the big expensive department stores. Those women are like harpies. And they get you when your knees are still wobbly from having glimpsed a price tag. Honestly, we've bought more ugly purses this way. Just avoid the big stores. It's far safer. Far. But just in case, here are a few lines we've found useful while shopping.

Things to Say to Skinny Ass Aggressive Salespeople When They Say "Can I help you?"

✧ Yes, please get me a soda.

✧ Would you mind rubbing my feet?

✧ Do you have any Xanax?

✧ Thanks, I'd love to borrow your house account.

✧ Did you notice that my pants are making your ass look fat?

Shelf Life of Underwear

Always shop for underwear by yourself. There is nothing less comfortable on a BFA than underwear two sizes too small that you bought because you were with your girlfriend and didn't want to admit how monumental your lump actually is. The great thing about underwear is that they don't charge by the yard, so go ahead and get a size that fits you. If the sheer humiliation and hopelessness of shopping in the lingerie department gets you down, buy men's underwear. The big ones.

A good pair of underwear can be made to last a lifetime. Originally it's nice and soft and new. After the first five hundred washings expect horrifying stains and broken elastic. These are now your emergency underwear and the pair you will wear the most since you never keep up with the laundry. As long as there is any piece of fabric strong enough to hold a safety pin, you have an available pair of bloomers. *Never* let people see your underwear (whether you are wearing it or have forgotten and left it hanging where someone will see it, like maybe, on the living room lamp). But if, by accident, they do . . . just tell them it's your dog toy or a bandage left behind by a wounded government agent. Here's another great tip about old underwear: you can also use them as a car cover.

Some of the Hurdles Involved in Sporting Sexy Underwear

Most styles are comprised largely of dental floss, turning spillage into a lethal weapon.

They roll up.

They roll down.

They bunch.

They itch.

They disappear.

They have been known to disappear forever.

That pair remains a concern.

Bra Fittings and Their Relevance as Torture

Sports bras are like bear traps. When you put one on it flattens you like a pancake so you won't bounce. Most B-FABs stopped wearing sports bras because we stopped working out a long time ago. Or we still work out, but we don't care if our boobs go up and down, which they don't because we'd never really work out that hard.

Thankfully manufacturers have improved upon the bra since back in the '50s, when they made women look like Fembots for Austin Powers (*The Spy Who Shagged Me*, "Yeah, baby"). Starchy bras used to push the breast into a freakish point, and then the girdle would stop all circulation beneath the waist. We've come a long way, baby. B-FAB Resolve: We will no longer wear girdles and stiff bras to force our figures into shape as if we were pork links. We will eat the pork links but we will no longer encase ourselves like them.

Another great tip is to always buy your push-up bras one size too large. It's a great place to store your spare tire. Simply reach down and firmly grasp your fat roll and pull it up, successfully augmenting your bust size. All without surgery! (See how much money you saved by buying this book? You probably ought to go out and buy ten to twenty more copies. Good idea! Thanks a lot. Great gift for friends who haven't yet noticed that they have a BFA.)

With any luck you thought that the above paragraph was a joke. But, in truth, in Janette's youth she created cleavage out of her stomach roll on more than one occasion, like the time she was doing stand-up comedy on a tour of U.S. military bases in Germany and England in a show sponsored by Miller beer. She had a green and black silk dress (weighted down with the inevitable oversized shoulder pads) with a plunging neckline that called for something better than a sternum. She got a very padded, very tight black bra and hauled as much of her spare tire as she could up into it. Dolly Parton stand aside! The best part of the whole night was the adorable little soldier who was besotted by them and kept coming through the autograph line over and over. He was charming, handsome, and particularly entertaining since she knew the knockers he was slathering over didn't really exist! It was very empowering. And now, with the advent of high-waisted Spanx, anybody can have a great rack.

TESTIMONIAL

B-FAB Marie

I was a store manager at Bloomingdale's. I was on a diet and had lost twenty pounds when I was called by our security guard to help apprehend a shoplifter. As I was running in my ortho-pedic shoes past the jewelry counter, I felt my baggy under-pants creeping down, down, down. I couldn't stop. I bent down while still running and scooped up my very stretched-out undies. Customers and employees were staring at me. I kept running. With my big ol' panties in hand we did catch that shoplifter.

If the Accessory Fits, Wear It

There are days when you might want to shop but just don't feel like facing the disappointment of trying on forty-two shirts that don't fit. On those days stick with the B-FAB standbys: shoes, gloves, and bags. These things fit *everybody*. Gloves are a favorite fat ass shopping item for many reasons. For starters, they are one of the only things, other than shoes, that you can find in a department store that always come in your size. Secondly, gorgeous gloves, if flaunted expressively as Audrey Hepburn does in *Breakfast at Tiffany's*, definitely take the attention off your ass. Put on a pair of really great, elegant, skintight, elbow-length kid gloves dyed banana yellow to match those amazing shoes you bought at the Presidents' Day sale, and people will think you're a size four. If one's gloves are expensive enough they fit like a glove. (That's not a stupid thing to say. Only expensive gloves actually fit like gloves. Cheap gloves fit like antique baseball mitts.) We're talking so perfect a fit you can still wear your rings. If you have gloves like that, we don't care how much you weigh. You're thin.

It's Not Hopeless, It's Your Face

No chapter of extensive research on the topic of fashion could be complete without mentioning the art of makeup. Most B-FABs put a lot of pressure on their kissers. This is due to the years of social torture we've all endured at the mercy of people constantly trumpeting "But you have such a pretty face." (Note: to all skinny ass people who tell us we have pretty faces, please know that all we hear is "If you could just lose your ass, you cow." Stop saying that to us or we will hurt you.)

That said, of course we B-FABs care how we look. Janette spends most of her time looking in the mirror, or the storefront window, or any polished metal surfaces such as the sides of butter knives. She thinks makeup is really a very important thing.

Without it, she asserts, a lot of women would have no self-confidence at all. You can tell if you read women's magazines that before their makeovers a lot of women were, you know, men. Which just goes to show that the makeup industry has been able to help a huge cross-section of Americans, including transvestites and cross-dressers. Makeup is also just fun. It's like finger paints for your face. You can transform yourself from that thing you see in the mirror when you first roll out of bed, into a much more brightly colored version of that thing.

Clothing and cosmetic styles change. We think the 1950s was the best fashion era for B-FABs. Marilyn Monroe was a superstar and, not only was she a size fourteen, she was considered perfect! Fashion then exemplified women at their best—curvaceous and real, not some waif-model with no sexuality or true female heat about her (not that we are judgmental in any way, because we're not). Maybe we'll never be Marilyn, but a whole heck of a lot of us are her size or bigger. So wave for the cameras and throw an air-kiss to all your adoring fans, you B-FAB movie star you.

TESTIMONIAL

B-FAB Anna May

Having grown up in an Italian-American family in the 1950s, when it was still considered desirable for women to look like women—this was before the Twiggy generation, when girls starved themselves to resemble the adolescent male body—I desired a big, round fat ass. We were in fact the last generation to yearn for the day we could proudly wear our full figures as a flag of our womanhood. Most of my aunts were large, full-figured women with well-rounded asses that jiggled and bounced when they walked. These women did everything with a passion and that included eating. They taught me not to fear food. It was a friend, not an enemy like it is today, and only by eating enough pasta could you achieve the perfect female figure. They had proof of this in the form of their favorite movie idol, bosomy, wide-hipped, full-figured Sophia Loren.

My aunts, like all Italian women, came alive at weddings; they danced with the men, other women, and, after a few glasses of wine, even by themselves. There was nothing timid about them. They knew how to have a good time and watching my aunts shimmy and shake while doing the tarantella convinced me that being a woman could be fun.

I was a chunky child. My chest was well developed by the time I was twelve and my ass was fairly large, but there was something missing: sadly, it had absolutely *no* shape to it! Unlike everyone I looked up to, who wore their bouncing cheeks with pride, mine were solid and flat on the sides and kind of pear shaped. For me there would never be that smooth, round basketball shape to bounce gently under my '50s-style, form-fitting skirt. It was a life-altering realization to know that I would never have a big round one. Now, many years later, I still lament my loss whenever I observe a beautiful, firm ass in skin-tight jeans and know that will never be me.

Counter Intelligence

LB: Co-Founding Member Confessional

recently found a fabulous new line of jeans that actually fit. I bought three pairs in black, brown, and navy blue denim. (Darker denim looks better on B-FABs than lighter denim.) They have a great name, too. They're called Tummy Tuck Jeans NYDJ—for "Real Women with Real Curves." I felt so lucky when I found those pants because pants rarely fit me and . . . I hate shopping! I especially hate looking for my size. I actually am frightened by numbers in general and what they stand for: clothing sizes, savings account amounts, birthdays, basically any table of measurements. To me math equations often resemble Egyptian hieroglyphics. If you were to ask me right now what eight times six is, I'd tell you that I haven't got a clue. I have to add up sixteen three times to get fifty-eight. I just did that on a Post-it. I confess that I have a block about math. Confessing that is an understatement, no matter how I say it. I was always the artistic one in school, with the words DAYDREAMS TOO MUCH DURING CLASS written in big red letters at the bottom of my report card. My favorite thing to do was stare out the window at the freshly mowed school yard imagining myself already on recess playing dodge-ball. I'm quite confident that my strident, fertile, and massive imagination kicked into high gear to escape the presentation of the dreaded math flash cards. I remember breaking out into a cold sweat just at the sight of them. To this day I only know my times tables up to five. Five times anything I can figure out. By the time I get to the sixes it becomes a blur requiring the use of calculators, fingers, friends, and 15 percent tip cards in my wallet.

This may explain my inability to count calories. Recently my dad bought me a kitchen scale, this shiny little flat metal device for weighing meat and fish. Are you kidding? I barely got it out of the box and I broke into a rash. How many calories in a potato versus au gratin? Chicken versus fish? It was just one of many immeasurable opportunities in my number-crunching world for me to become baffled—by recipe measurements, body measurements, body mass index, and all other communications that contain numbers. How many ounces in a quart? Quarts in a pint? I know you can buy a pint of ice cream. McDonald's has just outdone its own Quarter Pounder with the Angus Third Pounder hamburger. It took me a minute, but I think the Third Pounder is the bigger one. Is McDonald's messing with me? That would mean they took the burger from 25 percent to 33 percent, which is 8 percent more beef. I had a friend help me with that equation and it's still wrong. Anyway, how can a massive burger be sold in fractions? That seems to be a gimmick to sell more burgers, leaving consumers to think that they could be eating something else called a One Pounder, but they are watching their weight by eating a Third Pounder. Oh . . . my . . . God. (Actually, I gave up meat, and chicken, while writing this book.)

My counting handicap goes beyond food and flows into my workout schedule. How many days did I go to the gym this week? Two? Three? Not at all? Time goes by so fast, with errands and writing and hanging out and doing not much of anything, and then it's Sunday again.

Actually, I'm good at keeping track of one number. I am a size fourteen. Most of us are a size fourteen. What would most of us even do with a size zero? Use it as a dishrag? I can't even imagine one of my thighs fitting into that number. What mutant children are actually buying tiny clothing? Soap actresses? Triathletes? Not most of us. When I am at the local fashion outlet we're all eyeballing the larger sizes—walking sideways through aisles, checking out one another and the available larger-sized clothing at the end of the rack.

When, after much shuffling, I make my way into the dressing room, I like to try on everything all at once, filling an entire shopping cart with clothes. (That gives you a clue where I shop. They don't have shopping carts at Bergdorf Goodman or Saks Fifth Avenue.) Anyway, I always try to bypass the check-in lady because I hate the dressing room rule: ONLY SIX ITEMS AT A TIME ALLOWED IN DRESSING ROOM. I like to sneak by her so I can mix and match anything that, by some miracle, fits. It has to be the right price (i.e., cheap), the right color (not purple) and it cannot under any circumstances ride up my ass. If I'm lucky, one item will actually be comfortable, durable, and flattering. Of course, like a good man, this is very hard to find.

Suffice to say that my number phobia is very frustrating, especially when it comes to dress sizes. And now almost four pages into this essay, 978 words later I am left wondering, why do I live in a world of women who are at least a size fourteen and still think they're fat? Why can't we love being the size that we are? B-FABs are the majority. We are the power. Power in numbers.

Bonding with Your
Fellow B-FABs

 great friend can do a lot to take the pressure off your ass and goodness knows sometimes you feel that there's enough pressure back there to make you want to screech like a hoot owl. True friendships give you a chance to experience trust, to feel what it's like to be yourself, and to enjoy walking around without constantly having to hold your stomach in. Let it all hang out. Hanging out with your gal pal pack can make you feel less like a body of one and more like one among her B-FAB sisters. The real you, occasionally selfish, somewhat irritated, and very often bloated, is free to come out. Real comfort is seeing yourself reflected back in the eyes of your B-FAB BFF.

Great girlfriends through thick and thin love you no matter how much your weight goes up and down, as long as you're free to dine with them once in a while without your spouse. (Sometimes boyfriends and husbands interfere with the flow of natural girlfriend banter. Going out with your B-FABs also gives your man that chance to surprise you by cleaning the bathroom. Tell him how hot it makes you. Now go hit the Dairy Queen.) Friendship is a way to experience love. A best friend can make you feel safe, and heard and worthy. Kinda like the U.S. Coast Guard or a full package of Chips Ahoy! They are there to rescue you from yourself. (In fact this is a great time to plug the B-FAB Society. If you are short on friends—which is a condition that happens every now and then in life—get your own B-FAB Society local chapter up and going. Come to our message board at www.EmbracingYourBigFatAss.com and meet people. Friendships can be formed at any age and we all need a big ol' bucketload of BFFs to see us through over the years.)

The Beginning: Baby Be My Friend

Best friends are like dogs. They offer unconditional love and support and often follow us around wherever we go. For most of us, calling our closest friends a lifeline would be an understatement. Often we are closer to them than we are to our families and spouses. We started looking for friends when we were much tinier people, with our backsides bumping into one another in the school yard. One day, maybe during dodgeball, you threw the ball and some redhead named Margie caught it. You smiled at each other and, suddenly, you had a new best friend. Within an instant you had become one. You walked home from school together that afternoon and confided in each other about how big the sky seemed on a moonlit night or how your favorite color in the crayon box was midnight blue. After that, every day was all about finding your best friend in the hallway between classes to pass her a note or share an eye roll, constantly finding small activities to bond you ever closer. The fact that she existed made everything better.

Your Girlfriends Are Your Best Rearview Mirror

Now, let's fast-forward to where bonding over favorite crayon colors is a thing of the past. By the time you're in your teens it's all about boys and clothes and the forevermore favorite question between friends, "Does my fat ass make my fat ass look fat in these jeans?" That's the question that separates the BFFs from the crowd. A real friend will say the jeans look great if they do. Otherwise she'll tell you to try on a different style or at the very least, suggest that you pair them with a poncho.

B-FAB Laura's best friend growing up was a girl named Sue, who was about Laura's same height and weight. (One didn't make the other one look bigger.) Laura was always with Sue—at the pizza parlor, at the mall, hanging out at Sue's house, walking to the pool, listening to music, or doing absolutely nothing. A true friend is someone you can do nothing with and still have a great time.

Janette, on the other hand, always seems to go for gorgeous girlfriends. She likes beautiful women. They are so much more fun to look at than ugly ones. There is a classic thing where they say that gorgeous girls always have fat girlfriends. Maybe it's the other way around. Maybe fat girls like to get gorgeous girlfriends. Maybe we have more in common with them than you think. When Janette was in her twenties in acting school, she had a drop-dead beautiful, stunning girlfriend. Her name was Stephanie Phillips and she looked like a cross between Elizabeth Taylor in her *National Velvet* years and Ava Gardner in her days with Frank Sinatra. She weighed approximately one pound. They were in the same acting class and within a matter of months did everything together. True, Janette spent an awful lot of time listening to Stephanie's boyfriend stories when she had no boyfriend stories of her own, but that was hardly Stephanie's fault. They used to walk everywhere. Stephanie introduced Janette to Colombo Frozen Yogurt. (This was back in the '70s when frozen yogurt was new and cutting-edge.) It was before cell phones, and pay phones still cost ten cents. Stephanie would never let you spend a dime. If you so much as tried, she'd shove them back in your purse saying, "Save them for phone calls!" Every three or four blocks Stephanie would check her answering service to see if her manager had called in case an audition for something might have come up.

Once, in an acting class, someone came up to Janette and said, "Stephanie is so gorgeous. How can *you* be friends with her?" It was shocking. Janette felt terrible—as if all the oxygen had left her body for that one moment. She knew what the person was really asking, "Mustn't dowdy, chunky, plain Janette feel even uglier next to such a beauty?" Luckily Stephanie came back to her seat next to Janette and the conversation ended. It was crap. Janette felt great with Stephanie. Stephanie didn't judge Janette or concern herself in any way with Janette's looks. She just liked her. They were friends. They were planning to be big stars together. This proves that even non-B-FABs can still make great BFFs.

Things to Do with a B-FAB BFF

Take a break from feeling self-conscious.

Feel beautiful.

Pig out.

Go on a juice detox fast.

Connect with your best self.

Avoid your mother.

Numb and Number

You can't separate friends from food—it's the excuse to get together. "Hey, Linda, want a hamburger hoagie?" What is better than to go out and eat and talk with your BFF? Absolutely nothing. That's how we stop stressing—we eat comfort food and we converse about the day's activities, making sense of our senseless jobs, boyfriends, husbands, children, pet gerbils, money problems, and, yes, even our asses. Commiserating with a girlfriend over the size of your ass is just one of those things we have to do. It's like *Sex in the City*, only about your ass.

Eating out with one girlfriend or a pack of hungry B-FABs is the best way we know to go completely unconscious. We cannot possibly think about the real problems in our lives while sharing a sizzling plate of zucchini fries with beer chasers at T.G.I. Friday's. It's always the weekend there so you can completely forget the fact that you were about to go on a diet. With your BFFs you can feel as beautiful as you think you are.

One thing that no one, under any circumstances, should do

is suggest to a B-FAB that she might have gained weight or that she may want to consider going on a diet. You could very easily lose her friendship. That's because you have offended her. Not by calling her fat but by assuming that she doesn't have a mirror. It implies that she doesn't know that her pants don't fit—even her boots are tight—and that she is not already doing every freakin' thing she can to deal with it. Friends don't call each other fat. That's B-FAB Code.

Girlfriends support each other wherever they are in their individual journeys. If you want to lose weight, your friend should support you. If you don't want to lose weight, your friend should support you. If you want to go back to school, or learn how to draw, or construct your own Native American ceremonial sweat lodge in your backyard, a real BFF will get behind your behind. It's your life. Your friends are there to make living it more fun!

Girlfriends as Dates

Never underestimate the power of a great girl date. It's all the fun of dating men but without all the neurosis, misery, and hidden angst. You still get to dress up and the good thing is your girlfriend will appreciate it. Men don't really care if we wear old tablecloths. All they want to do is take them off anyway. As to the finer points of appreciating Italian leather shoes . . . again, trust to your BFF for that.

The following looks like poetry, but trust us, it's not. It doesn't always rhyme and the meter is wrong but we like the point. Just like your ass—it's not perfect but you accept it anyway.

THE LENGTH OF THE SHOW

Don't complain about how you overeat
As you grab another sweet.
Along the way find life's true passion,
No matter the way, the cost or the fashion.
Find friends to keep the rest of your life.
Not a husband, a mistress, a lover or wife.
Because asses are like boyfriends, they come and go,
But girlfriends stay for the length of the show.

The Secrets of a Fat Ass Date

JB: Co-Founding Member Confessional

I can't think of chocolate fondue without thinking of the Park Avalon Restaurant in the Flatiron district in New York City, which sounds like I'm not sticking to the subject but I am. I had my first chocolate fondue there and it was wonderful and a certain portion of it still resides on my BFA. I was there, at risk of eating that fired-up chocolate, as a duenna. (A duenna is: 1. An elderly woman who has charge of the girls and young unmarried women of a Spanish or Portuguese family. 2. A chaperone or governess. 3. Laura's friend.)

The reason I was at the Park Avalon was to meet a blind date, not mine. The date was for Laura but she didn't want to go alone, which sounds crazy if you didn't know that Laura and I were working on an article about online dating. Laura was far more shy than I. That meant I had to go along with her on her dates as an official third wheel. I felt like an octogenarian with a bad hip watching over the nubile princess. Laura towers over me. Laura does in all honesty think she has a BFA. She's gorgeous but, since she doesn't know it, she's just like the rest of us with BFA mentality. Don't for God's sake tell her that she's gorgeous—it might go straight to her ass.

Laura was a flirt-master of the highest caliber in those days, and the minute the man appeared, she would turn on all of her considerable charm. This resulted in me growing shorter and fatter as the date progressed. No matter what I wore, I was dressed in black.

To be fair, these dates were actually a lot of fun except for the part when the man was there. Laura and I would meet up so we could go to the date together and we'd one-up each other on horrifying expectations about the man we were going to meet. We'd name the men we were dating. Code words that we'd refer to again and again. The one we met at Park Avalon we called Grapeless. That was because he owned a wine distributing company yet he also had no chin. Even still, Laura was aglow.

Laura is like something on *Star Trek* when it comes to men. When you put her near them she starts to glow. They come at her like moths—they can't help it. She actually was in a *Star Trek* movie. Every time I see *The Wrath of Khan* on cable I watch it to see her as the Navigator. I always yell, "There's Laura!" It's enjoyable. Now you can do it, too.

So we're at a table and Laura is mesmerizing Grapeless—laughing, blushing, looking up through her eyelashes. She throws her head back shaking it just the right amount and laughing like Brigitte Bardot. My thighs pop out on either side. My BFA runs over to the side of the chair. I flag down a waiter with one hand while I mop up the water that I spilled in an attempt to divert the attention from my luxurious draping ass.

Laura, kittenish, makes Grapeless taste her Manhattan to see if it isn't just a tad too strong. I frantically order the chocolate fondue saying that I need it fast—a medical condition. Grapeless leans forward to canoodle in her ear. The fondue arrives. I eat it all. Every last drop.

Eventually I tie my ass cheeks into a giant bow in front of me and Laura and I make our escape from Grapeless. She wonders if he will call her or if he was appalled by her nonexistent BFA. Of course I want to beat her around the head and shoulders and shriek, "How can you even be thinking this?! He was besotted. He was drooling. He's probably already left you four messages. *And* you're gorgeous!" But that's when I realized that whatever I thought about Laura's looks . . . she was constantly judging everything about herself just like me and all the rest of us. So, B-FABs out there, we shouldn't judge our B-FAB sisters just because their BFAs aren't as massive as our own. The truth is that the beauty of the ass is *not* in the eye of the beholder. It's in the eye of the ass owner. It's what you see when you look in the mirror that counts. I probably should have said all that to Laura at the time.

SECTION V

A Working Woman with a Waddle

Your Job with a Bouncing BFA

Even though jobs are fraught with fear, boredom, and tight underpants, they are a necessity. The money we make keeps us fed and clothed. Whether you are blessed with an office window surrounded by city views or a cubicle with carpeted wall dividers, at least you are gainfully employed and probably earning more in a year than most people in third-world countries make in a lifetime. Stop complaining and start manipulating the situation to your advantage. Remember the great quote by John Gray, "You can only get what you want by loving what you already have." So, love your job, love your desk, your briefcase, the tight pantyhose and undersized suits and shoes you slip into for the nine to five. Repeat over and over to yourself, "I love this crappy place, I love my scratchy clothing, and I love my occasionally overly perfumed, brown-nosing coworkers. I love my paper-cut-driven existence. I love redundant collating, day in and day out, give or take a holiday or the death of a distant relative. I love my Big Fat Ass."

Hating Your Butt Cakes on the Job

The real problem is that you may be going to work with a poor body image. This can lead to an erosion in confidence—to thinking you're not worthy. Then your net worth suffers because you never get paid what you should. How on earth could your hemispheric butt make you less valuable to yourself and others at your job? See what we mean? You're nuts. It's not your ass, it's your self-loathing that can get you thrown out on the streets and penniless with a tin cup and a cute dog named Buttons begging for pocket change.

And if you manage to stay employed, forget that promotion. Why would anyone acknowledge you (give you more money) when you don't even acknowledge yourself? Your stupid ALV keeps saying, "I shouldn't go for that promotion. I'll never get it. I weigh more than the board of trustees." The moment you think your level of attractiveness should be equal to your salary you're opening up a cosmic Pandora's box. You have become part of the problem. Cut it out! You deserve that new paper route—as soon as you convince yourself of that fat fact. Now you stand a better chance of convincing everybody else. You may even upgrade from throwing local Penny Savers from your bike to becoming a UPS driver—it comes with an outfit.

Others Hating Your Butt Cakes on the Job

Let's say you've finally made peace with your piece (of ass) but coworkers continue to make you feel like crap. Judgmental looks and rolling eyeballs from fellow employees can get exhausting over time. You can't be trusted not to "go postal." Often we eat out of that nervous awareness that everyone else at the office weighs less than we do but makes more money. You feel like everyone is watching you as you devour lunch with the force of a Hoover vacuum. Cute, perky interns buzz around you, sizing you up, chuckling in the corner with another intern about your voracious appetite and rather large booty. Here's what we say: start saying to yourself, "Who the %#@ cares?" When you feel yourself speeding up as you walk past them, slow down and take a deep breath. Stop right in front of them at the Xerox machine and shake your ass in their face. Be proud. They are not better than you . . . and soon enough they'll be back on Craigslist looking for their next gig.

Lost in Oblivion

You may be committing an act of self-sabotage by carrying around an excess filing cabinet in your behind. As we have mentioned, there is a good chance you've been overlooked for promotions. (How could they miss you? You're standing right in front of them.) Thin, pretty people will always get better job offers the same way men still have an advantage over women in their earnings and advancement. This sucks because the more you get depressed over this fact the more you are likely to eat to get over it. It's like a Chinese finger cuff—you can't get out of it. Why do employers think physically more attractive people are smarter? There should be a law against such discrimination. Many people don't even overeat but they are overweight due to an underactive thyroid. For many it's genetic. The B-FAB Society should lobby for equal rights on the job. Let's say you are applying for a job as a beekeeper and they choose the thinner beekeeper over you; we say that's poppycock. Report them to the local police department. Sit on them until they hire you.

Snacking Kills Time and Makes You Smarter

With the prevalence of discrimination and self-hatred, the logical question is "Why don't we just stop eating?" Here's why—we have to snack on the job for survival! We are either brain-dead on a Monday morning needing a sugar rush, or bored out of our minds looking for anything else to pass the time. There is nothing like working as a secretary, therapist, nurse, or circus clown to work up an appetite. Jobs are so darn repetitive. Often the clock seems to stop moving as the day drags into that midday pit at 2 PM. How can you be expected to do the same activity all day long without breaking it up at least five times a day with little snacks: nut bags, a banana, M&M's? (You can also Xerox your ass.) Eating helps break up mind-numbing Mondays and helps you forget the fact that you wish you were dead. A late morning or afternoon snack can really charge up those brain waves. How can a boss expect you to think without a little nutritional sustenance? We feel smarter after a croissant chicken salad sandwich and we probably are. So lick every last crumb from the Saran Wrap, then wipe the mayo from your cheek. Now take on that next thought or confrontation in the boardroom, operating table, or three-ring circus. There's nothing like a little food to make you feel calmer before marching into your reed-thin manager's corner office to ask for a promotion or a matching 401(k) program. Sometimes biting into a leftover burrito you've stuffed behind your purse in that bottom drawer is exactly what you need. Calories give us courage. (Coffee works the same way in the morning. Beware of cranky B-FABs until after that first sip.)

Sick Ass Days

There may be days when you have snacked too much on the job the day before or maybe went out for martinis on a weeknight. On these days just call your boss and say, "I'm calling in fat. I'm tired. I need to work from bed today. Do you mind?" If he screams and says, "What, are you crazy?" get dressed and go in to work. At least you tried. They should declare a National Somewhat Chunky Day and let everyone who is even slightly overweight (by office standards) stay horizontal in bed at home watching Lifetime TV until late afternoon. There are holidays for other minorities, why not us? There's Saint Patrick's Day, Martin Luther King Day, Yom Kippur, and Chinese New Year. We need to declare ourselves because we are the majority being treated like a minority . . . only minorities get paid vacations. We need our own day in the calendar at least once a year—the Big Fat Ass Babes Day. While we're at it, why don't we throw in three weeks paid vacation, twenty-one sick days, and well over thirty-three fat days per year. It just makes sense.

Diversionary Tactics During a Big Ass Presentation

Did you give up searching for a rich man to marry you, and since you're fairly smart, went from waitressing and/or life as a hooker to an office job? In that case, we need to discuss situations where you may need to be in front of the room making a presentation. What if you start to lose your audience? If you feel yourself begin to panic and go into a flop sweat, do the following: First, make sure everyone is in proper viewing position. Stand up, turn around, and show them your full figure. Artfully strike a pose by putting one hand on your hip, with your weight on one foot more than the other, then wiggle just a tiny bit. Throw your arms up in the air and go into a big, long sigh and stretch. Reach for that pointing tool and smile gracefully as you go over flow-charts. Slowly turn around and stare into their eyes. Go into a *cucaracha* dance for a couple of seconds. They will see how much you enjoy your body with your robust sense of humor and everyone will want to buy anything on your flip chart or support you in your latest massive project. You've successfully employed your best diversionary tactic. A Cheshire cat grin at this point will complete this maneuver. Always remember, you need to be the one to liven up the workplace—they don't call it a "bored room" for nothing.

If you want to break the ice in a meeting that is a bit too serious, we suggest you start while flipping the chart and writing these words with your marker: "What do you think of my Big Fat Ass?" You'd be amazed at how memorable a meeting you can create. (Maybe, before you start, just draw a little picture of your ass in the upper right-hand corner. Use a laser pointer to occasionally reference your drawing.) Divert their attention to it (the small ass drawing) and say, "Remember, I do have the power here, no ifs, ands, or butts about it. Riggght? Ladies? Gentlemen?"

Office Parties

Very few people actually look forward to office gatherings under any circumstances. They're just an embarrassing nuisance. Nobody really has anything to say to one another, you never know what to wear, and you know you are going to overeat just to get through it. Often, a healthy B-FAB can be found in the corner of an office function holding up the wall. Who wants to go walking around the room saying hello and trying to strike up conversation with people they haven't bothered to get to know on the job so far, and if they did get to know they probably wouldn't like anyway? In fact, many B-FABs can be shy, and not so eager to impress with perfect designer threads and hourglass figures because we don't have the clothes and we do have the ass. We are the folks that actually do the work at the firm and are not so firm because of it. We simply ask to be left alone to do our jobs—not to have to politic at a party with public displays of our ass. Here's our suggestion: *Do* play the game. Buy a few key suits that make you look and feel like a million bucks. Stay after work for the office jamboree, Christmas party, birthday, etc. Position yourself sort of half sitting on the corner of your desk and just hold court. Have a friend get you treats from the buffet table and let everyone come to you. If it worked for Jabba the Hutt it can work for you, too. (Okay, we could have found a more realistic person than Jabba the Hutt, but we think that's funny.)

Why don't we try to take the opposite approach? Why shouldn't we be the life of the party? Forget worrying about what you look like to other people. Damn, bring on the pu pu platter. Turn up the music. Let's dance. It doesn't really matter why the office is adorned with streamers and confetti. Retirement, Hanukkah, New Year's, or Presidents' Day—who knows what day it is? Just know that where there is a party there's free food, and where there is free food there is alcohol. (Who knows, maybe you could get lucky with that cute boy from the tenth floor. He's been peeking at you as you walked by for months. Slap on a sexy dress and bring home a boy toy. Consider him your Christmas bonus to yourself. Unwrap him like a gift when you get home. Batteries not included.)

The Mother of All Examples of a Fat Ass Job Well Done

Commanding an audience at an office party requires that you believe that deep down you are dripping with charisma. There are many examples in history of fat people being the most powerful people in the room. Examples include Marlon Brando, King Henry VIII, Eleanor Roosevelt, and Santa Claus. But the greatest example, the real Queen of the Fat Ass Babes, was none other than Mae West. She used her assets on the job as a performer in every way possible, flaunting, in words, clothing, and style the fact that she was a powerful, man-eating B-FAB. How can you not adore a woman who came up with the following legendary quotes: "Cultivate your curves—they may be dangerous but they won't be avoided"? Here's another one: "She's the kind of girl who climbed up the ladder of success wrong by wrong." B-FAB Mae West can teach us everything we ever needed to know about getting ahead on the job. Here's some history: In the 1920s, she was too plump to become a flapper, the more popular female type of her day. She created her own film projects set in the nineteenth century so she could wear corsets and full-length gowns to hide her massive back-end equipment. To offset her chubby-cheeked face she wore giant feathered hats and tons of exotic jewelry. Being all dolled up herself wasn't enough; she used to darken the teeth of other women in her stage productions and films so she could come off as the only one with that Colgate smile. (Try this at your day job.)

Alternative Moneymaking Options for an Industrious Fat Ass

What if you're just weird and can't hold down a job or hate the idea of a nine-to-five? Quit while you're ahead with your behind—become a reality TV star. You can audition for *The Biggest Loser*, *The Tyra Banks Show*, or *Celebrity Fit Club*. Even better, create your own television network, "The Fat Ass Network." One of the first shows could be titled *Worth Your Weight in Gold*. The idea would be to bring together twenty contestants and watch them overeat. At the end of the month, they'd step onto a giant scale. A B-FAB host, maybe Mo'Nique, would then announce the winner, giving them gold bricks equal to the weight of their fat ass! Another great show could be called *She's a Brick House*.

Here's another show concept where the lard in your pants plays into the equation: For every pound you lose you make a hundred thousand dollars. The show is called *Meal or No Meal*.

You'd choose a picnic basket from a fat ass babe model standing on a huge stairway in embarrassing outfits next to other B-FABs. If the basket when opened says "MEAL," you eat that week. If it says "NO MEAL" the contestant gets no food until the next program. The winner who loses the most gets the money in a big blowout finale at the end of the season. Some may faint from malnutrition and be carried off on a stretcher. Those folks are definitely not the winners. The rule of *Meal or No Meal* is that you have to remain upright to win.

More Entrepreneurial Concepts

You can start a business in the self-help industry in a field related to the ass. *Entrepreneur* magazine and any good classified section in your local hometown paper are loaded with opportunities. Even adult education courses at a community college can get an industrious B-FAB's business plan started. Launch a flower basket business, a consultation by phone service, buy an ice-cream truck, or become a food critic and get paid to eat. Why not come up with something showing women how not to give a rat's ass about their asses anymore? Create motivational CD programs like Tony Robbins's. Create CD programs in your spare time that repeat subliminal messages over and over again that people can play at night before they fall asleep. "I love my fat ass. I love my fat ass. I see myself bathed in golden sunlight walking away from all the negative people in my life looking at my fat ass. I see all the mean, screwed-up people from my childhood and ex-boyfriends who ever hurt me walking away. I am a beautiful B-FAB. I am just as pretty as my little, thinner sister or friend." And so on, and so on. Then package the fat ass tapes and sell them in the back of the *National Enquirer*. When folks respond to your 1-800-EAT-LESS number, sell them more CDs, then a newsletter, and finally a subliminal music tape (Yanni) with an embedded message played backwards: "Ass my love I."

Another idea is to create motivational speeches and seminars and charge people a fortune to get in. Lecture for hours upon hours in cramped hotels in exotic destinations. At break time, charge the attendees $9.95 for a ham sandwich. Then after you're done speaking they can buy your CDs in the back of the room. The big breakthrough would be to teach B-FABs to walk across a bed of hot barbecued briquettes. Get portly participants all pumped up and screaming at one another, letting out their pent-up rage about not being the perfect size. Once everyone is possessed with the spirit, revved up, and "fearlass," they take the plunge and walk for sixty seconds across a bed of red, glistening chicken cookers. When it's over everybody's happy because their feet didn't burn and they had such a breakthrough. They shouted the magic words as a collective, *"We will never feel fat again. We will never feel fat again!"* Do this until 2 AM, then everyone passes out from exhaustion and is ready to buy whatever it is you want to sell them. The next level course should start at about $4,995. Cross-sell them on a continuity program offering them automatic shipments of hot coals directly to their door every month to remind them of this breakthrough experience. It's the "Hot Coal of the Month Club."

Silly concepts, you say? Not really. People are actually creating seminars every day. How about a Fat Ass Vacation Club? Clothing line? Smoothie drink? (If you think of any really good

ideas, feel free to contact the authors of this book on our website: www.EmbracingYourBigFatAss.com.)

Turn Your Ass into Your Asset

Not interested in joining the boom of infopreneurs and seminar
creators? Then just go on TV. Many industrious women are
making money in the broadcast media with their rear ends.
Study commercials for your *own* big break as the spokesperson
for something like "Pork, the Other White Meat." Take Kirstie
Alley, for example. She didn't lose that much weight but made
a fortune off every pound by becoming the spokesperson for
Jenny Craig. (*Who is Jenny Craig anyway and why can't she speak
for herself?*) God bless Kirstie for shooting the moon in *Star*
magazine one too many times. One day she must have simply
woken up with the idea of turning her ass into an astronomical
income. First she created *Fat Actress* on Showtime. (You go
girl!) Then her book came out and then the Jenny Craig deal.
After that she went on *Oprah* wearing panty hose under a bikini. So, although we don't want another diet program that we
won't stick to, we do like the idea of making money off your ass
as Kirstie did. We think it's a great idea when you can turn your
ass into a cottage industry. Put yourself on YouTube.com working out to the Pussycat Dolls. Create viral marketing like *The
Secret* and sell 750,000 copies of your DVD of yourself explain-
ing how you've discovered how to love yourself, then sell the
rights to Ron Howard and he'll turn it into the new version of
Cocoon. You might pick up a sponsorship deal with Tupperware,
or maybe get a makeover on *Tyra.* Flaunt your fat for that down
payment on your dream home. We dare you.

BFABs—Be Fireballs! Turn Up the Heat

Throw out that old system of thinking and start playing the size that you are. Play big. Remember, you are not your skin bag. Show your boss that you have big plans to become partner, take on the flashiest accounts, the biggest banquet rooms, be the most likable veterinarian's assistant, the most amazing floral arranger—whatever it is, be the top gun in your profession. It's not about what you look like but how well you can articulate your thoughts while carrying around that butt unit. Refuse any kind of thin-person discrimination. Smash through the glass ceiling or push your way backwards—that is, ass first— through revolving doors while balancing lunch. Your B-FAB status tells the world, and most especially your boss, that while you work for him or her, deep down *you're* in charge. Management will take notice how you aggressively assert yourself in any situation, any elevator, any lunch cart. Companies know that heavyset girls have big appetites for success with none of that pretentious crap about having to fit into a size-six Norma Kamali pantsuit to get ahead. You can leave lettuce lunches and Starbucks latte midday snacks to those waiflike coworkers who always look like they are about to pass out. They *are* about to pass out and when they do, when their skinny ass heads hit their desks, you will have slipped in just in time to retrieve those abandoned accounts from under their noses. Envious, much smaller fellow employees will resent your power plays and attempt to yell, "Back off, fireball!" But there's no stopping you, our well-endowed friend.

Your ass makes you stand out. Flaunt all the junk in your trunk as you come and go from your desk. Like a diamond, uniquely round cut or pear shaped, hold your head up high as you march across the room. (Some women have to pay thousands to have specialized Brazilian butts attached by plastic surgeons, but you've got all that action going on in the back naturally.)

In All Sincerity

In the words of Richard Austin Smith, "Even for the neurotic executive—as for everyone else—work has great therapeutic value; it is generally a last refuge, and deterioration there marks the final collapse of the man." Isn't that intense? We love it. We also feel that these kinds of quotes in the book make us look smarter. Bottom line—when it comes to a vocation, find something you like to do and do it. Period. Love yourself while doing it. It doesn't matter what it is, or how difficult it is or how simple it is. It only matters that when you get up every morning you are going somewhere you want to go. Work is important. How you spend your time is important. Do whatever you can dream up—except lap dancing . . . your boss would never let you out of his office. Break free of a place or a boss that makes you miserable. We're all pretty screwed up at work. Let others have their compulsions, let them push your buttons. Don't react. Act. Check into your own world with a good set of headphones and your downloaded favorite tunes. Break the mold. It's easy. Just sit on it.

B-FAB Betty

My ass has seen its share of bumps and bruises. Freshman year of college I was working on scenery at a summer stock theater in New Hampshire. The corner of the stage had been removed and replaced by a full orchestra. It was the end of a long day and I was eager to finish up and go off for a cocktail and dinner. The only chore left to do was to sweep the entire stage. I eagerly started on one side at the edge of the four-foot drop. Unfortunately, I was moving at a rapid pace . . . backwards. I took a last step back and fell ass first right off the stage into the orchestra pit, slamming my right cheek into the sharp corner of the wooden piano bench. *Oouch!!* My fall was also broken by the drum set. People came running. After I was untangled from the tympani with the help of my coworkers, they stood me upright and I walked around to catch my breath. My large, soft ass had taken on most of the impact of the fall, and I walked away with no other injuries. (Thank God for a fat ass!) However, sitting down on the right cheek was definitely not an option. The next morning I took a look in the mirror to check out the damage and oh my God . . . a bruise to end all bruises, perfectly in the center of my right cheek. By the end of that next day the bruise completely covered the entire cheek and began growing down my thigh. The color of the bruise ranged from a deep purple in the center to a lovely powder pink around the outside edge. The folks that rescued me from the drum set asked to see it, and when I reluctantly lifted my shorts, both their mouths dropped wide open in astonishment. For the next month people would come up to me and ask to see my ass. My ass continued to turn all the colors of the rainbow. I never thought I would show off my ass in public as I did that summer.

How My Big Fat Ass Paid the Bills

JB: Co-Founding Member Confessional

don't know about you but I've had it with worrying about what everybody else thinks of me and my billowing behind. Ever since my job ended on *The Rosie O'Donnell Show*, my Big Fat Ass has been haunting me. I'm not suggesting that I didn't have a Big Fat Ass while I was working on that show, just that Big Fat Asses were more acceptable there. Many of us enlarged upon our asses during our tenure at 30 Rockefeller Plaza. I, for instance, gained fifty pounds during the first year and a half. I blame the audience for only getting up off the couch long enough to put more incredible, wonderful, fattening, BFA-exploding food into the mailbox. I also blame PR firms for sending M&M's, chocolate-covered potato chips, and free marzipan.

My big rear end has, on the other hand, been useful to me in my career. For instance, on my cooking show, *Lighten Up!*, which aired on the Food Network, my gigantic BFA became part of our programming. When we were taping the pilot, we had a camera run-through in the morning just to make sure everything looked perfect. We had a rehearsal where all the producers and directors and Food Network development people told me and my cohost how great we looked. Then my boyfriend, Barry, sidled up to me and said, "Don't let them shoot from behind. You can't turn your back and walk to the oven because the camera broadens you so much and, trust me, neither of you are going to be happy." Basically I heard it as, "Your ass looks like the Hoover Dam." Hmmm.

I didn't actually know what to do about our massive cans but I did tell my cohost, the lovely and talented Christina Deyo, that Barry had said we looked like sofa butts (BFA Rule: Always exaggerate.) I told Christina to just play along because I almost had an idea. By the time the Chicken Parm Roll-ups were ready for the oven so was I. I simply told the audience the truth. I informed them that we couldn't turn around to go to the oven because then they'd see our enormous back acreage and that that would not be good for anyone. I also reminded them that, as everyone knows, the camera adds 5,326 pounds. Then we backed our way to the oven, which became our signature "Butt Walk." Throughout the series we kept coming up with new ways to get to the kitchen equipment behind us without exposing the viewers to more than they could handle. If you are ever on camera, never turn around for any reason. Just back away. There is no reason to flap out what no man should rightly see. "Man" in this case referring to the species *Mankind homididibus* . . . what do they call them? *Homo sapiens*. (Also known as *Homo fat-assians* in scientific circles.)

I am a compulsive eater who had become a spokesperson for all things thin! The cooking show launched my short run as a weight loss role model, which was very taxing considering that I am fat. I became the editor at large for *First for Women* magazine. I had my own column with my picture on it and everything. The column was called "Winning at Slimming with Janette." I also became a spokesperson for Molly McButter, the fat-free butter substitute that I really do like and no I'm not still working there. I was a frequent guest on the local news in New York and on *The Wayne Brady Show*. I was constantly showing my "fat" picture in public and, in private, obsessing about how to hide my BFA when I was on TV.

There was a lot of pressure to pretend I didn't have a BFA. I went on Weight Watchers and lost weight, so for a while I only had an MFA (Medium Fat Ass) but alas, my butt is my bumper crop again this year. It's turning my jeans into an instrument of torture. The problem is that a little extra snacking for three or four hours at a stretch without stopping for a year and a half and, suddenly, I have a nice fat roll hanging over the snap on my jeans. It's a metal snap. I'm allergic to metal so now I have a refreshing, bubbly rash on my fat roll. You see how life can catch up with you? Make this a Lesson for Living and never let your fat roll run your life. Get a pair of loose pants for God's sake and get rid of those damn jeans. Right now, at five three, I weigh 161.3. I know exactly because, as a gift, my sister got me a digital scale (so I slashed her tires). It's one of those scales that also gives you your percentage of body fat. I am 40 percent fat! Sausage is 22 percent fat. I'm fatter than sausage.

Then, out of the blue, Laura called me up and said she had an idea for a book. I said, "What's the book about?" She said, "It's called 'Embracing Your Big Fat Ass.'" She invited me to write it with her and I got so excited I leapt to my feet and my thighs applauded. The best part about writing a book is that I get to spend time out of the city at my house in the country where I wear loose pants, ugly shirts, and underwear so big I get to use those rainbow-striped suspenders I've been saving for a rainy day. I'm going to write this book and have some snacks. I'll start with the snack. Whoops. (Not to worry. I just tripped over my BFA on the way to the kitchen.)

Working for Food

LB: Co-Founding Member Confessional

Food is a major source of both comfort and disappointment in my life. I'm often either thinking about it . . . or eating it. I'm rarely let down by its flavor; it's what it does to the size of my stomach that bothers me. I'm always ten to twenty pounds overweight but since I'm tall I hide it really well. I look best when dressed. Take me out of my clothing and it gets bumpy. I've always wandered aimlessly from food source to food source. Food is better than a good boyfriend with a nice ass. Okay, not really, but I do live for Lay's potato chips. Give me a bucket of salt. Due to my love of these rock crystals, I retain water like SpongeBob SquarePants.

Becoming a waitress was the perfect occupation. I felt safer near food. I wanted to serve meals to people for a couple of reasons: I had no other work experience and I could eat at a discount. Office jobs never really appealed to me. I loved the interaction with new people in a restaurant and the challenge of selling my customers more food than they could safely consume. My first job was at a place called the Wild Iris in Overland Park, Kansas. There were always cooking smells in the air with people coming in to share a drink and a meal and to leave me tips. Evidence of my newfound love of the Wild Iris started to show itself on my arms and thighs. But it was okay, I had beaten out all the other waitresses selling my customers every potential appetizer and dessert possible. I made it to the Wild Iris newsletter—tops in sales. I took my eight hundred dollars in savings and my brother's car (a taxi-yellow Gremlin) and drove to San Diego, to start my career in showbiz.

I got a job at a place that was actually called Skinny Haven Restaurant. Surely, one could stay thin at a place like this. But, no. I simply ate lots and lots of low-calorie food and stayed at my basic 165 pounds. Weight Watchers worked for about a year but I lost the calculator and hated the idea of belonging to any kind of society of people who turned food into a system and then attempted to keep track of it. It seemed pointless. I'm very bad at crunching numbers. (See the LB confessional "Counter Intelligence.")

I moved from Kansas to California to become the superstar I never became. But with that constant ten to twenty pounds of excess Banks I carried around, I couldn't compete with the likes of Daryl Hannah, Cybill Shepherd, and all the other tall, skinny, perfect blondes I was auditioning against in those frightening L.A. casting offices. I may have been somewhat pretty and talented . . . just not Hollywood-bone-thin-beautiful-and-talented.

I did find some film work. I starred in three independent film projects for this famous filmmaker guy, Roger Corman. We shot them in the Philippines. It was quite an adventure. I lost ten pounds of water weight while dressed in leather and leading armies into battle on the desert sands of Pagsanjan. I was on the Action Adventure Diet. I also had a small but highly visible role in *Star Trek II: The Wrath of Khan*. My success in films stops there. Once I had a featured guest role on television's *T.J. Hooker,* hosted a show on the Sci Fi Channel, and was Maxine Headroom for Cinemax. There. Now you know my résumé.

Why was I such an underachiever in Hollywood? Did I fail at nepotism? Did I not sleep my way to the top with the right people? (I could never figure out who were the right people to sleep with.) I think the reason I didn't work that much in Tinseltown is much less tainted than that. *I think I could never cross over to the big time because I was an actress that actually ate.* I loved my big breakfasts with bacon, toast, and Tater Tots.

Fortunately, I discovered radio and writing, two media where my full face didn't matter. I also discovered sunglasses. Anybody looks good in shades. It makes your face cheeks look less like a woodchuck. Sunglasses are fun for everyone. At the end of the day, I am proud of who I am, the work I have and haven't done . . . and every squared-up and rounded-off inch of me.

SECTION VI

Attempted Health and Weight Loss Projects

Dieting Sucks Because
Baby's Got Back

One thing seems apparent. Diets don't work. They turn us into cranky people. We are miserable while losing weight for two reasons: 1) Our blood sugar levels drop and we pass out. 2) We don't lose weight, and even if we do we are certain to gain it all back if we even think of eating.

We persistently go on fad diets. We must be crazy. After a starvation period of a few weeks or months our bodies weigh the same and sometimes even more than before. Lord Goodman (whoever he is) says, "Every so often I lose weight, and, to my utter horror and indignation, I find in the quiet of the night somebody has put it back on." Sometimes we go on diets because we want to be liked by others in high school, college, at work, or to become a beauty queen on a float in the Puerto

Rican Day Parade. We want to look like we care about what we look like in the mirror and to be able to brag that we understand how some diets work. Take the Zone Diet, for example: a person needs CliffsNotes to figure it out. Whether it's understanding a diet's methodology or actually going on a diet, we do it all to fit in—to fit into our lives, our heads, and our pants.

What's more fattening, the food or the criticism? One way B-FAB Janette found to keep her ass in check was to follow what she called "The 80 Percent Rule," which says "You don't have to be perfect, you just have to be better." Too often people get discouraged because they are reaching for some pinnacle of socially acceptable beauty that is really just making us all miserable.

No matter how thin you get, fat feels like it's always lurking just around the corner. And how about the way it can creep up on you?! One day you're looking good, your stomach is . . . well okay, not exactly flat, but it can't be used as a weapon, either. If you stand at an angle and suck up your diaphragm you look really good. You get a lot of compliments and sometimes even, kiss of death, a great boyfriend. (*What* is more fattening than that?) Next thing you know, bing, boom, bam and you start getting spillage again, and then, before you know it, you accidentally give away every pair of pants you own that aren't sweatpants or drawstring. Suddenly you find yourself using Chunky Monkey as dip for Oreo cookies and thinking, What's one more buttermilk biscuit? By the time you realize it's happened you've gone up five dress sizes (again) and you feel like you're starting all over. But you aren't starting over. You are just starting for the 4,747th time. What an accomplishment! Congratulations. Good for you!

Oh My God, I'm Getting Married and Other Reasons to Starve Yourself

Class reunions, birthdays, family reunions, new jobs, and other horrifying events can make us want to get that popular Kate Moss emaciated look. Weight loss regimes are acts of complete desperation, often undertaken before significant events in our lives. We shout out, "Oh my God, he proposed. I have to stop eating!" Weddings are the worst time to stop eating—energy levels plummet and mood swings skyrocket when you eat nothing but carrots. This puts you in an almost constant state of PMS, which could then turn you into Bridezilla. If you insist on losing that extra ten pounds, do it way before the wedding shower, like the year before.

Maybe you're not getting married. Maybe you slam head-on into an ex-boyfriend in the street or you walk into a great sale at Macy's. You simply had to buy some sexy little black dress marked half off. Forget the fact that the zipper doesn't close— New Year's Eve is two weeks away and you have nothing to wear! So on December 15 you convince yourself to live off of lemonade, cayenne pepper, and maple syrup. Well, come December 31, the dress fits but you're still miserable. Why? Because deep down you still feel like a fat person. By March the dress will be shoved to the back of the closet, reminding you of how New Year's resolutions never, ever work. Let's take a look at what we do to ourselves and our bodies while we're trying to lose weight.

TESTIMONIAL

B-FAB Mary

"I caught a side glimpse of myself in my sister's full-length bedroom mirror. I was horrified and in that moment understood why I don't own a full-length mirror. I had just turned thirty-five and my boyfriend and I had split up, so the only place where I felt I could gain some control over my life was to go on the South Beach Diet. Everyone was raving about it, so I took the plunge. After eight weeks friends and family had stopped making mean remarks about my ass and I looked great. We were headed for the Christmas holidays and I was determined to bypass the extra mashed potatoes and turkey stuffing at my mom's house. Well, it didn't exactly work. I gained it all back by mid-February. I pulled my larger pants from the place I had hoped to bury them in my closet forever. I call it the Resurrection of the Fat Pants. Now, I sort of walk around knowing I'm overweight but refusing to go through the highs and lows of a diet anymore.

What's In a Name?

We B-FABs torture ourselves on fad weight loss programs to get a sense of belonging. Often diet brands are designed with names of glamorous places so we can imagine being whisked off to these glorious hot spots like Hollywood, the Mediterranean, the Hamptons, or South Beach once we finally lose that weight. This is also why they don't give diets the following names: the Bronx Cheer Diet, Three Mile Island Cocktail, or the Bowery

Bowel Recovery System. It seems like no matter how many diets we put our bodies through, with some fat years and some thin ones, we are still always left waiting for our lives to change miraculously and for the fantasy to begin. Pills and powders, blended beverages, and weight loss machines and systems are sending the message, "Wait until you're thin . . . and watch your life begin. Your once upon a time is now. Go on our plan and not only will you have a tiny waistline and beautiful behind, you'll also receive with this special one-time offer . . . the perfect new husband, and dream vacation. Your life will be filled with wonder and complete, unending happiness. Call now, operators are standing by."

Alternative Activities to Going on a Diet

⟡ Try Clairol's Shine Happy. Your hair looks gorgeous for weeks.

⟡ Have sex with your boyfriend and actually enjoy it.

⟡ Figure out how to sell your stuff on eBay Express or Amazon.com.

⟡ Book your New Year's Eve in the Caribbean now with a few girlfriends.

⟡ Spend hours in front of the mirror determining a new side part for your hair.

⟡ After that second date with that great new guy, send him one hundred thank-you e-mails.

Push Yourself Away from the Table

Tyra Banks says, "I love all kinds of bread. Whenever I crave junk food, I want salty things like peanuts or potato chips. I love food and feel that it is something that should be enjoyed. I eat whatever I want to eat. I just don't *overeat*." That may be hard to conceive. That's because the only escape most B-FABs have from pink slips and fickle boyfriends is to eat to excess. On top of that, we all have this guilt plowed into us by our parents, who said, "Someone's starving somewhere. Damn it, eat!" So, we'd lick our plates clean to help an orphan somewhere, then go to our room and play with Barbie. As our thighs and backsides grew larger, deep down many of us started to hate our skinny ass Barbie dolls. Young B-FABs everywhere rebelled by disfiguring their Barbie dolls—lighting their hair on fire, pulling the heads off, and sticking them in the microwave. (Destruction of skinny ass dolls can be very gratifying.)

Keep It to Yourself

Diets are like shoes: the soles get worn out and they get kicked to the curb for that new hot set of stilettos. One day you'll be on the Liquid Diet, the next wasting away on nothing but bacon fat. Who needs it? It's torture. On the other hand, by simply reducing caloric intake you may, by some sleight of hand, drop a few pounds. Do not tell your friends you are dieting. That's too much pressure. Simply say, "I'm not on a diet—I'm just ordering tomatoes instead of potatoes." Just leave a little food on your plate even if it turns out to be seconds.

Don't Die-it, Try It

Here's another B-FAB tip: try anything once. As our Grande Dame B-FAB Mae West said, "I'll try anything once, twice if I like it, three times to make sure." Go to the gym once, sleep with that guy once, and dip your finger into the chocolate fondue fountain once. If you try every fattening food in the world once, it's not likely you will die of morbid obesity. We suggest that you choose one day out of every week when you will allow yourself your favorite yummy food in whatever massive quantities you desire. That's what Elizabeth Taylor does—she eats whatever she wants one day out of every week. She said, "When I diet, I diet—and when I have an orgasm, I have an orgasm." We really don't know what this means but we like it. Having almost died over ten times and with seven ex-husbands, she's living proof that self-indulgence works.

So, to recap: We are not *dieting* anymore. Maybe we'll eat a little less salt. (Try Spike, it's a great natural seasoning.) The truth is, to actually hang out with us you will need to swear the following: "I, So and So, will never go on a diet again." (Call any future weight loss plan a "program.") If you said this out loud just now then welcome to the B-FAB Society! Your Big Fat Ass Bonus Gift and User's Guide will be arriving shortly. If, upon initiation, you are coming off a diet of some kind, it's important to regain your energy by eating carbohydrates. Did you try the Atkins Diet? If so, we are very sorry. Here's how the Atkins Diet works: You will have bacon and cheese omelets for breakfast, lunch, and dinner. Lose ten pounds in two weeks! ("Yippee! It's working.") Stay on it for another two months, at which time you could very well have started to eat your own muscle mass. ("Oh, crap, I'm fainting at board meetings again.") You start eating carbs again so you can stay upright. Then the weight comes on faster than before and you put on fifteen pounds in one month. ("I'm going to have to kill somebody.")

There aren't that many diets on the market. We could only come up with a few:

Abs Diet

Atkins Diet

Blood Type Diet

Bob Greene's Best Life Diet

Body for Life

Cabbage Soup Diet

Cayenne Pepper, Molasses, Lemonade Diet

Dean Ornish Diet

Dr. Phil Challenge

eDiets.com

Fat Flush Diet

Fit for Life

Flavor Point Diet

French Women's Diet

Glycemic Index Diet

Grapefruit Diet

Hamptons Diet

Hollywood Diet

Japanese Women's Diet

Jenny Craig

L.A. Shape Diet

L.A. Weight Loss program

Living Low-Carb Diet

Mediterranean Diet

NutriSystem program

One Day Diet

Perricone Promise

Picture Perfect Diet

Pritikin Diet

Richard Simmons Diet

Scarsdale Diet

Six-Day Body Makeover

Slim-Fast Diet

Sonoma Diet

South Beach Diet

Step Diet

Sugar Busters Diet

Suzanne Somers program

Three-Hour Diet

Trim Spa

Weight Watchers program

Zone Diet

Pay Attention to the Man Behind the Curtain

Here's another reason why dieting is so hard—glossy offerings in magazines and multimillion-dollar commercials on TV lure us to eat. To stay out of diet mode, stay aware of the brainwashing that goes on in the media. They sell us pills, powders, and packages that arrive at your door with a Magic Bullet blender. Start to notice how TV commercials are turning us into a bunch of food-obsessed, snack-craving fanatics. These spots switch incessantly from one minute to the next, back and forth, from weight loss products to fast-food eateries. They show us close-ups of juicy burgers followed by infomercials about weight loss shakes. What's a girl to do? They put the juicy steaks and pies, fries, and sundaes practically up against the camera lens so we can get lost in every juicy morsel. As the spot ends we are left sitting on our couches dazed and confused and salivating. Then the show we were watching comes back on and all we can think about is that close-up of a hamburger. After watching one of these fast-food commercials and making a subsequent run to the drive-thru, a perfectly good day of dieting can be wasted on a night binge. Don't you love shrieking into a clown face (speaker) while you're stoned, *"I said, I want a Big Mac and double fries. I said 'fries' not 'flies'."*

The laws of advertising should be changed. After all, they outlawed liquor ads on network TV, figuring out that tempting drunks to go drink could very well increase our prison population. Cigarette spots were done away with, too, because it turns out cancer is not so sexy after all. Go figure. Aren't junk food ads just as bad, just as dangerous to a population of B-FABs trying to get by? Cut us some slack here, media people. Don't make us come out looking for you. That's why we believe that coming together with a very public Big Fat Ass Babe Society is the answer. Let's reclaim our power over the golden arches. Did you know that the colors red and yellow make you subliminally want to eat more? Did you know that KFC puts a noise at a high-pitched frequency in the background of their spots that only kids can hear that makes them want to go visit the Colonel? (This is true. We saw it on the local news.) In summary, control your urge to put your body through another yo-yo year. Try the TiVo plan.

Once you have decided not to waste your time dieting anymore you can finally find something that works. The simple solution: find food that is both satisfying and light enough to keep your fat ass in a more manageable condition. That's what Janette's cooking show on the Food Network was all about.

Janette's mac and cheese recipe was written up in *Fitness* magazine in an article titled "5 Top Chefs Share Favorite Light Recipes." Top chef. Janette. We're not bragging . . . we're just saying. The magic behind her mac and cheese is that it is about half the fat and calories and more than double the fiber of traditional mac and cheese. It actually has vegetables cooked right in it. (Remember, we're all supposed to have at least five servings a day . . . That can be a challenge so Janette tries to disguise them into something good.)

Janette's Mac and Cheese

---

vegetable cooking spray
12 ounces dry elbow macaroni (3 cups dried)
½ cup white wine

4 red bell peppers, seeded and deveined, cut into thin strips

2 medium yellow squash (about a pound), cut into thin strips

2 medium Vidalia onions, chopped

1 clove garlic, finely chopped

1 tablespoon salt, plus more to taste

1 tablespoon butter

2 tablespoons flour

2 teaspoons dry mustard

1 cup skim milk

½ teaspoon dried thyme leaves

freshly ground black pepper

16 ounces part-skim ricotta cheese

¼ cup grated Parmesan

¼ cup bread crumbs

Preheat the oven to 325 degrees F. Spray a 2-quart baking dish with vegetable cooking spray, set aside.

Bring a large pot of salted water to a boil and cook the macaroni until just tender, about 8 minutes. Drain, rinse under cold running water, and return to pot.

Meanwhile, heat the wine in a large nonstick skillet over medium-high heat. Add the bell peppers, squash, onions, garlic, and 2 teaspoons of salt. Cook until tender, 10 to 12 minutes, adding a little water if more liquid is needed. Drain the vegetables in a large colander set over a bowl. Add the vegetables to the pasta and set the juices from the vegetables aside.

Melt the butter in a small saucepan over medium heat. Add the flour and mustard and cook, stirring constantly for 2 to 3 minutes. Whisking constantly, slowly pour in the milk and the juices from the vegetables. Add the thyme and 1 teaspoon of salt. Cook, stirring, for 4 to 5 minutes. Season with additional salt and pepper, to taste.

In a large bowl beat the ricotta until smooth. Slowly fold in the white sauce. Toss with the macaroni mixture. Transfer to the 2-quart baking dish and sprinkle with Parmesan. Sprinkle bread crumbs over the top and lightly spray them with the vegetable cooking spray. Bake until top is golden brown, about 35 minutes. Serve immediately.

YIELD: 6 servings

PER SERVING

477	calories
10.9	total grams of fat
6	grams of saturated fat
7	grams of fiber

Here's Janette's entire cooking secret: Replace fat and increase fiber. Replace processed white flour with whole grain flour. Whenever you read a recipe, just key in on the fattening ingredients and experiment with healthier replacements. It's just that simple. There's no reason to give up fettuccine Alfredo. Just find a new way to make it. Janette did.

Janette's Spaghetti Squash Alfredo

1 large spaghetti squash, about 4 cups cooked
2 teaspoons olive oil
1 large white onion, chopped
½ cup fat-free cream cheese

½ *cup reduced fat sour cream*

½ *cup grated Parmesan cheese*

1½ *teaspoons of salt*

½ *teaspoon of freshly ground pepper to taste*

4 *large sage leaves, finely chopped*

¼ *teaspoon freshly grated nutmeg*

Leave the spaghetti squash whole, piercing the skin a few times with a thin bladed knife or a skewer. Place in a microwave-safe bowl and cook on high for 13 to 15 minutes, rotating the squash once. Remove from microwave. Let cool a bit then cut in half and remove the seeds. Use a fork to pull the strands loose. Set squash aside and discard the skin.

In a large nonstick skillet, heat the olive oil and add the onion. Cook until the onion softens and becomes transparent, about 5 minutes.

Add the cream cheese, sour cream, and Parmesan cheese. Heat through, stirring to blend well. Add spaghetti squash, salt and pepper, and continue to heat, stirring gently, until spaghetti squash is hot. Add the sage and nutmeg, stir well, and remove from heat. Serve immediately.

Note: For an even more fattening-tasting Alfredo sauce stir in one tablespoon Molly McButter.

YIELD: 4 servings

PER SERVING

204   calories

  9.1   total grams of fat

  4.4   grams of saturated fat

  3   grams of fiber

Diet plans will try to razzle-dazzle you. Save the money and go to the movies. Buy the small bag of popcorn while watching a romantic tearjerker. If you must add butter, just go ahead but don't add more when you're halfway through the bag and it starts to get dry. (It's not really butter. We don't know what it is.) Buy flavored water instead of a Coke. Resist the gummy bears, Goobers, and Raisinets. As Erma Bombeck said, "Never order food in excess of your body weight."

My Life in Diets

JB: Co-Founding Member Confessional

I know everything there is to know about dieting. I have been on almost every diet they've ever marketed and I've lost approximately 1,337 pounds in my lifetime—so far. (I am B-FAB. Hear me roar in numbers too big to ignore.) As of this writing I weigh . . . hold on while I take off my shoes . . . and my watch and my rings and my glasses, my socks, and who needs that underwire? Just a minute while I take off my pants. Okay. Don't peek. I weigh 161.3. (That may seem high to you but it's low for me.) I have the best of both worlds. All the attention and satisfaction of having lost all that weight plus I still get to blame everything on my ass.

Here's the truth about diets. They all work. For a while. If you follow the Beverly Hills Diet and eat nothing but fruit— you will lose weight. I had sores on my mouth on pineapple day and got queasy on watermelon Wednesday . . . but I did lose weight. Weight Watchers, Fit for Life, the Cabbage Soup Diet. They all worked for me. I weighed 115 pounds when I was seven, 200 when I was twelve. I was 250 by the time I was fourteen and at around twenty I weighed 275. This may not be the average B-FAB experience but it was mine.

It's impossible to know me or even meet me for more than ten minutes and not know how much I used to weigh. It's so much a part of my identity that I have to let people know about it even if they never knew me when I was heavier. I'm proud of it. I'm attached to it and defensive about it; "I am *too* fat." Also, if I'm honest, which quite frankly I hate to be, I also mention it so frequently to make up for the fact that I'm still no Tinker Bell. I can keep a hundred pounds off. Anything after that is yo-yo.

I started dieting in eighth grade. I grew up in an old farmhouse in the middle of 148 acres with my divorced father. We had no friends, no neighbors, no relatives, no TV, and no record player. No one ever came there. For five years I was alone with my father, my sister, and my great-aunt Martie. My father trained us well. He would say, "Never trust anyone. Everyone is out to get you. They all want what you have. You can't trust anyone but me or your sister." Then I got to school and I trusted no one and spoke to no one so everyone made fun of me because I wouldn't talk. Later on, as I doubled in size that first year, they started making fun of me for being fat.

I wanted to be accepted so I started to diet. At first I made up my own—anything from the starting-tomorrow-I'll-never-eat-again diet to the nothing-but-boiled-eggs system. These attempts didn't last long and I always ended up gaining more weight in the long run. When I was a student at Temple University in Philadelphia I reached my peak weight. In the dorms they called me "Moby Judy" and "Wall to Wall Janette." At that time there were about 30,000 students registered with only about 3,000 of them living on campus. The dorms seemed to house mostly football players, cheerleaders, and of course me. I was unhappy, even unhappier than in my isolated childhood. I had always eaten to hide from my misery, but in Philadelphia in the early '70s I hit a new low. I got so miserable . . . I couldn't eat. It was fabulous!

I started my red-letter diet—I call it the Dormitory Diet. One morning I went through the line at breakfast and no one was more surprised than myself when I came out at the end of the line with nothing except a scoop of scrambled eggs and three glasses of grapefruit juice. The rest of the day I didn't even want to eat. I quickly became obsessed with not eating. It was every bit as consuming as eating had been. As soon as a week or so had passed I started my countdown, "I haven't eaten anything but eggs for eight days." As the weeks went by my counting became more elaborate. "I haven't eaten anything but eggs for one month, two weeks, four days, and seventeen hours." I was, to put it mildly, boring. My roommate deserved a medal. I would quiz her endlessly: "Sylvia, guess how many days has it been since I ate anything other than an egg? Guess how many hours? Sylvia? *Sylvia?*"

At first just not eating was enough. I felt better than I had in months. Remember . . . Moby Judy had been very depressed. I'm certain in retrospect that my mood lifted because I had found one thing I could control—as long as I was unremittingly rigid. Within days not eating started to have predictable results—I started losing weight. My pants were looser and I could feel ever so slightly better about myself. This made me focus on how big a payoff I could get by starving myself. I wasn't upset. I felt in control and on top of it. I lost fifty pounds in two months. Then I got greedy to lose weight even faster and stopped eating anything. I drank two glasses of grapefruit juice in the morning. Seven days later my "willpower" deserted me. (I never believed I had willpower anyway. It felt like I just got lucky and woke up on a diet.)

The next year I fell madly in love, not that I ever told him. He was even nice to me. We were friends! Then we had a fight. I was so upset I couldn't eat. It was wonderful! It may seem a little extreme but it's a lot faster than Weight Watchers. Even now I will occasionally say to my boyfriend, "Barry, sweetie, if you really loved me you would dump me like a hot rock and break my heart so I could lose all my weight." (Of course once I was thin and beautiful I'd expect him to come ask me out again.) The point is, it's easier to be brokenhearted than it is to stick to a diet. My broken heart helped me shed another fifteen big ones.

I didn't lose any more until about a year later when I started the diet pills. They're just speed. It was right after college. I always say, "I did speed once every day for a year." But it was probably longer than that. I must have taken it for at least two years. (Those years just flew by!) I hardly slept at all especially at first. I'd lie there in my very shoddy first apartment on Diamond Street in North Philadelphia with my heart beating in my ears in a kind of twilight exhaustion that wasn't quite sleep. I would usually dose off at around five or six in the morning. Then I'd get up at eight feeling like I'd been beaten with a stick. I'd immediately take my pill. I would go with my girlfriend Anne Marie. She was incredibly beautiful and sweet . . . and she had a car. The doctor's office was easy to find since it always had a very long line of nervous women snaking out the door and up the block. We'd get in the line, which moved amazingly fast.

Once you got into the waiting room, every minute or so a nurse would kick open the treatment room door and shout, "Next!" When you got in it was an assembly line. One nurse weighed you, another one took your blood pressure. When you finally got to the doctor, he'd say, "You've lost ten pounds this week. Are you okay?" Of course he didn't really care and everyone said yes. He'd hand you an envelope of pills and you were out the back door and good to go. Back at the car we'd open the envelopes to see what we'd gotten: Christmas trees, pink footballs (my favorite), white crosses, or black beauties (which I hated). I got down to around 150 pounds. One hundred and twenty-five pounds lighter than the first day when I only ate eggs and grapefruit juice.

Every morning I'd swallow a pill and fall back down on the bed or into a chair for a half hour. It used to feel to me like I was a train chugging and laboring to make it up and over a steep, steep mountain. At 8:30 AM exactly thirty minutes later, every single day for a year . . . I crested the mountain and started to fly. *Everything* was interesting. I would talk to anyone. I chain-smoked three packs of cigarettes a day. Food was not on my radar. Thank God I was young or my head would probably have exploded.

In my late twenties I moved to New York City and for ten years I went up and down between 150 and 170 pounds, following plans like the Bahamian Diet or Fit for Life or Atkins Diet. I did them all. Then in 1989 I got hired by an ad agency that paid me two thousand dollars to go on Slim-Fast. It was me and fourteen other women. We had to stay on the diet and come in every two weeks to have pictures taken in a hot pink leotard, *no stockings*. Nothing could have been better motivation to stay on that diet. I lost twice as much as anyone else. Here's how I did it: I cheated. We were supposed to have a Slim-Fast shake for breakfast followed by a Slim-Fast bar and glass of skim milk as a snack. Then you were supposed to have another shake for lunch followed by a "sensible" dinner. I had a better idea. The bars had fewer calories than the shakes so I thought the first thing I could do was get rid of those shakes! I ate the bars, but I thought, why drink milk when water has less calories? A sensible dinner for me, for five months, was a dry baked potato and green salad with vinegar. I lost fifty pounds. Then I started fainting. The first time I passed out I was staying in Maryland with a boyfriend that I had landed. I was outside his friend's house walking down the sidewalk and I just fell over on the ground. I got up after a few minutes but for the next week or so . . . I kept goin' down. I finally put two and two together and started eating again, after which I stopped fainting all over the place. I can't blame the Slim-Fast people. I was eating far less than they described in their plan. By the time I finished my version of the Slim-Fast diet, I was down to 127 pounds. That lasted for almost a week. It took eight or nine years for my weight to creep back up to 193. Since then it's been down to 166 pounds, up to 177, down to 149, up to 175, and now, drumroll, down to 161.3.

Due to some of the outfits in my closet I'd like to weigh 150 pounds again. But between you and me, I don't give a rat's ass. I do care that I eat the right things for health. I do care that I exercise and stretch so that I am still mobile when I'm seventy years old but otherwise I think I look fine. The way I see it, I'm getting a B in a subject that I used to fail. That's good enough for me. I'm tired of my weight being my whole life story. I'd rather just do the best I can and be happy wherever my ass lands. No drugs, no fads, no sleepless nights. Just me loving us exactly as we are. Me, myself, and my ass. The three of us.

Exercising Your Big Fat Ass

What's more attractive than a forty-plus B-FAB sweating her ass off on the rowing machine, huffing and puffing and damned if she'll admit that they had a point when her parents told her to quit smoking like a stack? Whenever you go to a fitness club there's always the temptation to compare yourself to all the thin, young, muscular chippies who live to work out. These annoying gym bunnies do deserve credit for how hard they have worked, but we don't feel like we have to be the ones to give it to them. Gym bunnies were mean to us. "Us" the little fat kids. We're over that now—of course we are! And we're kidding (kind of) because we know there are many good and wonderful people who love to work out—not that we know any. We, the authors of this book, commend them. We can't identify with them. But we do commend them.

Here's the Thing About Exercise

You have to do it. Really, you have to. It's not about losing weight. Even if you're stick-thin you have to exercise. It's for your health physically and now they are even nagging us to exercise for mental health. It's kind of annoying. The point here is that anyone can exercise and if you just start doing anything at all, it leads to more. You don't even necessarily have to be emotionally or physically ready to exercise. You don't have to have time to exercise. You just have to pick up a dumbbell. No matter how much you dread it, chances are you'll feel better after you've finished.

Exercising a Big Fat Ass is even more important than exercising a little scrawny one and here's why: if there's more of it to be seen, then you want it to look even better. There are all kinds of butt exercises you can do, such as that donkey kick

The Ugliest Shoes Imaginable Janette's favorite new butt exercise is walking in MBT shoes. She saw them in a magazine. They come from Switzerland and the initials stand for Masai Barefoot Technology. They are the ugliest shoes imaginable and quite expensive but the bottom of the shoe is round so you have to work to balance as you walk, which means you burn about 15 percent more calories and, more to the point, it specifically works your butt muscles. Janette has been walking fifty-four blocks four times a week going back and forth to work. Her butt thanks her for it. Laura's favorite butt exercise is riding a stationary bike at the gym in plain view for one of the Baldwin brothers. Any one of them. Well, not Stephen.

thing where you are on all fours and you bring your knee in to your chest then stretch it out straight behind you. That one isn't too boring. Walking up and down stairs is good for your derrière and so are squats and lunges—although who the heck wants to do that is more than we can imagine.

There is, in our minds, a distinction between working out and exercise. Working out sounds seriously difficult. It has the word *work* in it. We work enough. We'll just exercise. It can be moderate. We're into moderate. We don't want to obsess about it. We obsess about food. Isn't that enough? We want to be healthier not miserable-er.

It's More Fun If You Make It Sound Good

For instance, you could do as B-FAB Janette does and tell people, "I'm off for a run!" when actually she means she's taking a walk. It doesn't sound impressive to say, "I'm going walking!" Calling it running makes her feel young and athletic and basically in control of her life, but she really doesn't run. It hurts. If you have ever tried to run with a BFA you know that gravity has this odd habit of letting your ass go up with you, but your body comes back down first, leaving your ass to miss its mark and come down almost as far as the back of your knees before it bounces back up again and finally jiggles into place.

What If You Don't Want to Go to a Gym?

Even if moving doesn't come naturally to you, no matter how much you want to sit around all day on your lard lump, it's not good for you. For some of us that's horrible news (Janette). She has a fantasy where, in her perfect world, she becomes a brain under a cake dish like on *Star Trek*. Janette doesn't go to the gym but she does exercise whether she likes it or not. Do you think Janette *wants* to take a break from writing and drag her ass up the steep hill behind her house and into the woods where she walks around a path on the top three times? Do you think she *likes* that? Because you're nuts if you do. There are bugs everywhere. There's the omnipresent possibility of big dogs. One time she found a guy dressed in camouflage hunting wild turkey with his face painted. (This is how she knows she has a strong heart. She's not dead.) That damn hill walk is definitely tiring because it's steep—that's why it's called a hill. There is nothing to read. No TV. No snacks. Nowhere to put your feet up and let your mind wander. But she does it. Why? Because she still wants be able to walk up that hill when she's seventy-five. (We wish Janette had bigger goals but we don't judge.)

If we carry extra weight that's all the more reason to make sure we are as healthy as we can get. Exercise is separate from eating. It's like brushing your teeth—if you don't do it, they'll be disgusting, fall out, and do you no good at all. Then you'll look like poor Uncle Elmer visiting from Poughkeepsie. Same with your muscles. If you don't use them they will atrophy and get weak and nobody will want to touch you—except the handyman, but you have to pay him.

Joining a Gym

Walking up a hill is not always convenient, which is why the country is riddled with fitness establishments. There may come a time in your life when organized exercise is right for you. That means making the decision to join a gym. We've all been there and sometimes it works and you go and sometimes you join and don't even walk down that street again. It's a very personal journey for all of us. Most of us get the desire to start going to a gym after we've been overeating for about a year and a half until none of our clothes fit except for the ones that would also fit Gigantor the Magnificent. If you are joining the gym to lose weight, before you join you are most likely to try in the vicinity of five new diets. We recommend the French Fry Diet, the Pineapple Diet, the I Hate My Husband Diet, the My Job Sucks Diet or, one of our personal favorites, the Bolivian River Water Diet (Montezuma's revenge is *very* slenderizing). When all of those weight loss campaigns have led to a net gain of nine or more pounds, we may get desperate enough to join a gym.

Being Judged at the Gym

It's a good idea to find a B-FAB friend and just blab on about all the reasons you can't join a gym. You'll find that most of those complaints are just things you are afraid of—like worrying about whether other people will think you are working out hard enough. (So what if you took a nap between sets on the weight machines.) Here's the thing. It's nobody's business and is definitely against gym etiquette to have any opinion at all about anybody else there. It's a given that everyone will look their worst and not want to be there. Why should you be any different? So what, there's a scale—nobody will force you to get on it. If you think you're too tired to work out, just think how tired you'll be with no muscle mass and think how much less you'll be able to eat. (Muscle burns more calories than fat, so the more muscle you have the more you can eat without gaining more weight.) Maybe you hate the idea of being singled out in aerobics class. (Hey . . . you in the back . . . stop reading!) Who cares? You're paying them. This isn't school. They can ram it.

Paying for the Horror

The problem most of us have to face if we decide to join a gym is that it carries the prerequisite of working overtime or getting a part-time job to pay for it. Some great ideas for getting the extra cash include making your own line of homemade jewelry out of beads that you can guilt your friends and family into buying, selling your old shoes on eBay, and hiring your tomcat out for stud. Think of all the kittens he can father and all at a tidy profit. And imagine how happy you'll be making him. Animals are people, too.

Once you've come up with the cash, just stop by the gym and tell them you're thinking of enlisting. They'll immediately sweep you into a private room with a young, vibrant, healthy gym fanatic who will charm you right into feeling both old and fat. They will give you a hard sell even though you've already reconciled yourself to the fact you'll never be able to escape without joining. Just don't make eye contact. Stare at your Nikes. Don't forget your talcum powder.

The theory is that when you have to look at that $129 a month debit on your bank statement you will cart your big lazy ass to the gym. After all, you've paid for it. Alas, it's not always that simple. If we had all the money we've spent on gym memberships that we haven't used . . . well then we wouldn't actually need to be writing this book. Of course we'd write it anyway. Yes we would. Because we care about you and about your ass.

That's the kind of people we are. The kind of people who would rather go off on a tangent than even think about exercising our back forty.

The Gym Is a Great Place to Feel Bad About Yourself

Any fitness guru (we think) will tell you that you want to set yourself up to win, so it's a good idea to start small. Try "Today I will walk past my new gym." Eventually walking this new way will become part of your routine. Then you can start stopping in to the juice bar at the gym to have something healthy and green (although frankly, we prefer orange juice and a carrot muffin. That counts as a vegetable, doesn't it?) In no time at all you'll be considering going into the locker room and maybe even reading Us magazine in there.

What to Wear to the Gym

If you have gone so far as to not only join the gym but actually plan to attend . . . then you can look as horrifying as you want. The gym is the one place where you can go filthy, with dirty hair and a bad outfit and fit right in. Once you start exercising you can be very sanctimonious. Just by walking into a fitness establishment that you are personally paying (auto-debit) for, you automatically get so many brownie points that you can get away with everything up to and including black socks with white sneakers, outfits from Kohl's, and ill-fitting sports bras. Smelly is fine. Everybody at the gym is a little smelly. It's part of the experience.

On the downside, this is only true when entering the gym. By the time you leave you are expected to be clean. That often entails a trip to the shower. *We're sorry. We dropped that on you pretty suddenly there. Do you need a brandy? No? Alright, then we'll go on.* The shower. Yes. Home of fungus, mildew, and God knows what other fetid microbes. All we can suggest is that you have a healthy concern for infection and think before you sit. For example, when you walk into the sauna, swathed in towels, and feel its deep dry heat and see three nymphettes with perfect stark naked bodies, muscled without a sign of cellulite, sprawled out like they are waiting for a photographer from *Penthouse*— look at those gleaming cedar boards and remember they are gleaming because they have been worn down by innumerable asses that have come before you. If this image hasn't made you weak and sick and caused you to swear off saunas forever, just remember to layer twelve to sixteen towels before you sit. Spray yourself liberally with disinfectant every few minutes and stare down anyone who tries to sit in there with you. This way you should still be able to enjoy the experience with a lesser likelihood of catching scabies. (Don't forget to remember if you actually work out that every piece of equipment you touch has also been handled by every sweaty-disease-bag who ponied up the cash to buy a membership. Choose a really skanky gym and you could lose your appetite for hours at a time—consider this added value on your membership costs.)

In an Effort to Prevent Infection We Recommend the Following Equipment

✧ Hip boots for the shower.

✧ Rubber gloves for touching anything whatsoever, including your trainer.

◇ Purell hand disinfectant to use so frequently that gym employees think you have a condition.

◇ Rubber sheeting for the steam room.

◇ Lysol, Pine-Sol, and Midol (in case you have to pretend you can't work out because your cousin Marge is in town).

The other grave danger in the locker room is the naked-talkers: people who like to get starkers and then strike up a conversation. What do you say to a naked stranger? "Here, hold my watermelon." These naked-talkers stare you down. They dare you to look—but you don't want to. What on earth could you say? "How are you? Love your bikini wax!"

Actually Working Out on Occasion (Since You Have To)

The first thing that might strike you about using the exercise equipment in your new fitness club is how mind-numbingly boring it looks. Do not be taken in by this. It is, in fact, even more boring than it looks. Never underestimate the Chinese water torture aspects of your average treadmill. Like a gerbil in a wheel, a dog in an experiment, you are walking on a conveyor belt—keeping up with a machine.

There are lots of things you can do to make the time pass while sweating your BFA to a nub, speed-walking nowhere. One thing you can do is to choose a gym that has TVs. It usually takes your entire five minute warm-up to get your !%#*&^@ ear phones to work. Once you're pretty much up to speed, you can start channel surfing for something riveting enough to take your mind off how much you'd rather set your hair on fire than be doing this. Some of our favorite treadmill TV moments: Any shark attack at all—in fact any eating of anyone by any wild animal, monster, or alien is good because it's so compelling you won't even want to get off the stupid treadmill and risk missing a minute. The dinosaur attack scenes in *Jurassic Park* are great. The singing of the "Marseillaise" in *Casablanca*, as well as *Raiders of the Lost Ark*, *Star Wars*, and *Iron Chef* are highly recommended—you literally don't mind that you're sweating like a bull moose.

The Treadmill Is Not the Only Awful Thing You Can Do at the Gym

You can also go nowhere on a stationary bike for thirty minutes until your thighs burn like you're a survivor on that crashed spaceship at the beginning of *Planet of the Apes*—the remake. That's how bad you feel on that bike. Or you can ride an elliptical machine in case you always regretted missing the Spanish Inquisition. Another great thing you can try is lifting weights. Heavy things. For no purpose at all. (Except of course for bone health and to increase your metabolism.) In most gyms you have a whole floor devoted to machines ingeniously developed so that you can lift something with ease yet be totally crippled by pain the next day.

The Personal Trainer

Hiring a personal trainer is a great way to act out your S&M and bondage tendencies. This could really work out for you if you've always wanted to call someone "Dominant Master Sir" and have a secret, guilty attraction to pain and personal humiliation.

Personal Trainers Are

Younger than you.

Thinner than you.

In better shape than you.

Prettier (or more handsome) than you.

They have more self-discipline than you.

They are perkier than you.

They are more annoying than anyone.

In Closing

Research indicates—and if it doesn't, it should—that if you just keep flogging yourself on a daily basis to move a little more than you did the day before, anyone can improve their physical fitness. You can go to a gym if you want or just do it at home. Housekeeping and walking and taking the stairs all count. Buy a bike or take up swimming. Find something you can do that you don't hate too much. (Unless you already love exercise, in which case, go on to the next chapter.) We believe in doing as much as you possibly can without being overly miserable. Do your best, then praise yourself and have a snack. Isn't that right? That seems good. We're tired now from all this typing. This is exercise, too. Yes it is. Our fingers are in *spectacular* shape.

TESTIMONIAL

B-FAB Wendi

My nickname when I was young was "Mushy Tushy." That is what certain family members used to call me. It stuck in my head and I have thought of myself that way ever since and low and behold my ass followed right along. I come from a family of voluptuous Jewish women and I never knew anyone in my family who had a round, shapely, muscular bottom. So I thought it was my genetic destiny to join the ranks of my family's large, mushy bottoms. Later in life I acquired yet another name for my ass. I had a friend who said I was part of the "flat ass" club. You know, when you really don't have a booty, it just sort of hangs down, and continues into your legs. Not really an appealing picture, flat yet mushy. Two, two, two sins in one.

Now I'm forty-three and have been working out quite a bit. Having accomplished upper-body definition and relatively firm abs, I thought it was time to tackle the impossible. I recently made it my personal trainer's assignment to help me get an ass! (She, by the way, has an ass that you really only see in magazines; it's perfect. I never really thought an ass like that was real, but she has one. It's round, firm but still very feminine. It looks so good I often want to spank it.) So with lots of squats, lunges, and one-legged bridges that hurt like hell, I have been working on my bootylicious project while listening to "Shake Your Money Maker." I have another trainer I work with from time to time, a young man, and I told him about my build-an-ass project. He immediately said he'd like to be put on that project because, as he said, "You know I like me some butt!" So now I have two trainers dedicated to my ambitious goal of having a real butt, one that has shape and curve.

The other day I promptly jumped up from having coffee with a girlfriend and asked her to check out my ass. She said it does look more round and lifted—she said it had some curve to it. I'm not sure, she might have been humoring me so that I wouldn't be discouraged, but I'd like to think that my mission impossible is not so impossible. Something must be working because my husband just told me the other day, very enthusiastically, that my ass looked great!

Leaving It All Behind

Managing Fat Ass Sprawl
on Trips of Any Kind

B-FAB travel, whether for business or pleasure, is often complicated. Some people get to leave their luggage in their rooms, but we have to carry ours around with us. Vacation for us might involve logistics. B-FABs are far less likely to jet round the world with nothing but a carry-on. We need lots of spare shoes, for one thing. On vacation, what with all the sightseeing, shopping, and getting lost, we spend much more time on our feet, which, quite frankly, hurts. This is not a time for high heels and narrow toes. Get yourself lots of nice cushioned shoes like Merrells or Clarks. Shoes that are flat on the bottom and prepared to hold you up. But shoes aren't your only problem. Traveling is a pain in the ass—just packing and facing the sad reality that, no matter how full your closet is, you have nothing to wear. Everything is too big or too small or too ugly or too out of style. Of course you don't notice this until your suitcase is lying open and empty on your bed and your plane is leaving in four hours. We strongly recommend packing everything you own including your goldfish and your Gold Bond powder. It's a vacation. How much fun will you have if you get a thigh rash? See what we mean? Trust us. Pack heavy.

Vacations can be far more stressful than business travel. You have saved up *all year* for this. You had better have fun. Lots of pressure. Vacations make you stop working. Then you get anxious about not working, so you overeat. The closer you get to the end of the vacation the more you worry about going back to work and the fact that none of your pants will button. At this point you are probably getting pant panic attacks. You might even wonder if travel is worth it. The answer is "yes" for two reasons. One, if it's business travel, your boss is making you do it, so you have to. Two, if it's vacation, it's a chance to pull your attention off criticizing yourself and your ass and to focus instead on the many horrors of modern-day travel.

Fitting in the Airplane Seat

This is a challenge for most of us. No one wants to have to call the flight attendant and say, "The plane doesn't fit." Is it starting to get a little tight as you force yourself down between the armrests? Here's a quick tip from someone who's been there: *Do not attempt to get up quickly once you've wedged yourself in!* On the other hand we do feel, personally, that the cheesy-ass airlines could make the seats bigger than the ones we remember from preschool. Some of those planes have seats that could quite honestly be recycled to people who collect miniatures.

If you find you are pumping with your arms (either to get in or out of the seat), stop fighting your fanny. Look your seat-mates in the eye, smile broadly, raise those armrests, and adjust your pulsating posterior. Get comfortable. A comfortable ass is a happy ass. If the lucky sons of guns who got the window and aisle seats don't have BFAs yet, they soon will, so give 'em a taste of how it's done. A true Big Fat Ass Babe flies proud with her ass held high.

Frightened Beyond Belief: Your Bathing Suit

Vacation can be a scary time since your so-called friends and selfish family members are constantly insisting on taking vacations near the ocean, like in Saint Croix or Fort Lauderdale. Some others prefer the wide white beaches of the Carolinas or the majestic sands of Maui. Some people think of no one but themselves. We're not saying that being by the water isn't nice. But it does have a serious drawback. You are expected to wear a bathing suit. A horrible stretchy thing that clings to your body, exposing every bulge and ripple of cellulite. And this is supposed to be relaxing? (Janette handles this problem by not wearing a bathing suit. Ever. She swims in a dress. It's just more comfortable for her. Odd. But more comfortable. People always tell her not to be silly. They tell her nobody cares. She cares. Leaning back on a lounge chair and eyeballing your varicose veins is less soothing than you might expect.)

There are some people who just can't envision themselves out of the water. These "friends" are equally likely to rope you into a vacation at some overcrowded hotel in the desert where you can spend the entire afternoon, "At the pool!!" In case you have forgotten for even an instant that you have a BFA, there will be plenty of ill-mannered pool rats pointing it out to each other at the top of their miserable little twelve-year-old lungs. Aren't kids cute?

When it comes to swimwear, it's best to just pretend you fell in the pool wearing your clothes. Once you're wet you might as well stay in and have a good time. Choose a lightweight outfit that won't make you drown. Sure, you'd think you'd be safe to kid around with lots of people watching but they'd probably think it was part of the entertainment and there you'd be, dressed like Marie Antoinette, dead in the bottom of the pool. Thankfully, we're here to warn you. When you get out of the pool, immediately change into light casual linen pants and a big shirt. FLAX has a great loose-fitting line that can be found in boutiques or online. Swim only once. Doggie paddle to the side of the pool, get out, go to your hotel room, order room service, and never come out again.

Should you be so advanced a B-FAB as to not give a rat's ass what anyone thinks and to feel no need to wear extra clothes, we say, You go! That's spectacular. Just be understanding of your B-FAB sisters who would rather hear the F-word at 120 decibels than the dreaded phrase *bikini*.

In-Room Minibars and Packing a Refrigerator for Your Room

Just because you are on vacation doesn't mean your midnight cravings will be any less. Minibar prices being what they are, we suggest you bring some sandwiches. Egg salad on white bread with a leaf of iceberg lettuce is an old family favorite. Bologna is also good and Janette loves olive loaf. It might be pig snot solidified but she doesn't care. She likes it. On a kaiser roll with yellow mustard. All kinds of sandwiches are good, from pimento loaf with Velveeta to peanut butter and bacon on whole grain with honey; the main differences are that some need to be kept cold faster than others. That's why you need a refrigerator in your room. Remember to eat your most perishable sandwiches first, ideally in the middle of the night because you can't sleep because of the time change. That makes you really hungry.

Some of the newer, bigger, snazzier hotels now have what we call "guerrilla minibars." If you remove an item for more than sixty seconds, you have to pay for it. Why, we've spent upwards of three and a half minutes just sniffing around the package ends on a Toblerone with no intention of going to second base (unwrapping). This is an outrage. We suggest you carry some trail mix or a Baby Ruth bar in your purse to give you the energy to get over this hurdle. Paydays are also good and never forget the glory of an Almond Joy. It's mostly coconut. Isn't that a fruit?

Dog Days at the Day Spas

Day spas are the perfect place to go to escape the water sports your loved ones crave. Let them go out there dressed in rubber bands and spandex. You can spend a calming day getting your hair, face, body, nails, and feet pampered. B-FABs don't often excuse themselves from life for a whole day to get buttered up but we recommend you consider it. You'll become a much more likable person and with enough spa time, you could relax and actually become bearable—maybe even give up therapy. You might even be able to upgrade your intimate relationship from the one you have with your pet ferret to being with an actual human. Let your friends and loved ones wallow by that pool. Let your husband wear a Speedo that's so tight he gets gangrene. You don't have to know about it. You're at the spa. No one calls you fat at the spa. No screaming. No children. Ahhhhh.

When you first walk into a day spa you just get all dreamy. They design it that way with fabric walls, candles, rounded furniture, nice smelly things, and the sound of chimes. For some reason chimes and spiritual music are big in these joints. It's great—acoustical sounds mixed up with the cries of breeding wolves, Native American drumming, and a midget dancing on a windy beach performing a bell solo are just a few of the great CDs you can expect to discover at your vacation day spa. As you walk from treatment room to treatment room you wonder if you've died and gone to someplace Beyoncé lives all the time. There are no mirrors so you don't have to catch a glimpse of yourself hanging out in the day spa robe and matching slippers, thank God. Scents of lavender and rose water waft up your nose while you listen to Enya singing "Orinoco Flow (Sail Away)." Notice how your BFA just recedes into the background (where it belongs).

Destination Spas—Two Tickets to Paradise with a B-FAB BFF

If you really have had it with standing in line at Disney World and feeling like Dumbo by the pool, maybe you could take your own vacation with a B-FAB girlfriend. You can get to a destination spa by car, plane, donkey, or zephyr. A destination spa just really means it's a fancy resort in an exotic location. There are hundreds of them around the world. They're a pain in the ass to get to and often cost your kid's college tuition for a week's stay, but keep in mind that sending your kid to college doesn't get them nearly as far as it used to.

When you travel with your BFF, leave your spouse behind. You would just annoy the hell out of him by ignoring him completely because you are far too busy drinking watermelon juice and getting mud packs and seaweed baths. Sex is out of the question because rarely is there any point of entry since you're so often wrapped in something like a towel or rice paper.

Tips for Trips for Girls with Hips

If you are traveling for business you'd better pack everything you own, hoping at least one outfit will work and still fit for that big presentation. Just expect a bad hair day. It's easier that way. There are some rules of business travel: Stay in four- to five-star hotels with king-sized beds. The key to big deals on the road is to feel like a big deal yourself at all times. Request upgrades to premium suites with those afternoon appetizers set out for only those folks on the *special* floor—the one you are on. Only certain card keys can even get you onto those floors. Schmooze with other Big Deal B-FABs in the reception area with the flat-screen TV, fruit bowls, and tables set with linens and fresh-cut flowers. Here again, this is a wonderful opportunity for free food.

If for some godawful reason you can't go deluxe, try out places that overfeed you with carbohydrates at their free continental breakfasts. Red Roof Inn has a good one. Coffee and orange juice flow like a river. They offer up the standard, classic choices: bagels, muffins, cereal, toast, and oatmeal. Feel free to smear that bagel with tons of Philadelphia cream cheese (protein). Don't forget to use the cool automatic bagel slicer. The only hindrance may be the huge line of families all waiting to use one of the two toasters, but they do give you a nifty set of tongs so you can pull your bagel out once it's done. Other big fat tip: Stand near the toaster. When it's done sometimes the toast shoots across the room, or you may encounter the rotating toaster oven where bread spins round once and shoots out the bottom. Be careful some other babe doesn't make off with yours. There is absolutely nobody on a diet here. You cannot count calories. Take some of the butters up to your room.

Getting Your Mind off Your Ass in Vegas

Las Vegas is a Mecca for fat asses everywhere. It's a first choice for business travel and it's also a great place to go on vacation because when you start walking through the casinos and looking around, you realize that B-FABs have overtaken the world! Everybody has a fat ass and cellulite, so right away we can feel at home. (Note: skintight double-knit polyester is not the only way to go. See the fashion chapter for tips.)

The great thing about Vegas is that there is so much to do to keep your mind off your ass. There are lots of great restaurants. Janette loves Craftsteak in the MGM Grand. She also recommends Spago downstairs at Caesars and, as long as you have an emergency number for your doctor, brunch at the Wynn. It is possible, we believe, to suffer a stomach rupture if you go back to the buffet too many times, so we caution you to pace yourself.

If food is not enough to distract you from your ass, why not see if you can lose your shirt? A disastrous day in the casino can make you forget you even have an ass. Your bulbous butt will be the least of your problems once you don't even have cab money for the airport.

In the end, vacations, like bathing suit cover-ups, need to be designed to suit you. Go to foreign countries where they appreciate full-figured women. Try Italy for instance—you'll get cat-calls. Try the spaghetti and meatballs. *Mangia.*

Getting Frisked at the Airport

JB: Co-Founding Member Confessional

As a B-FAB, I'm not at all fond of being handled by strangers. I don't even touch myself. I like to get dressed, do my best to cover every lump, and then forget I have them. This is no longer possible—at least not at airports. In our post-9/11 world you can be manhandled at will by the TSA. Here's what happened to me: I was at the airport checking in. When they asked for identification I gave them my driver's license. The license had expired. While it was certainly a significant detail, it was one I hadn't noticed. I'd gotten the license in my teens but I don't actually know how to drive. I live in New York. Many New Yorkers don't drive cars. I'm not sure how to make the car go. I'm confused about whether you push on the gas pedal when you turn the key or just turn the key. I am also afraid that if I turn the key the car will leap forward like a wolverine out of the night, possibly crashing through the garage door. This makes it clear that the last time I tried to drive they didn't have push-button windows yet, so why expect me to have noticed that my driver's license had expired?

Hagarella, the airline check-in girl, did notice and she got right on her speakerphone. Have you ever seen *Silkwood*? The movie with Meryl Streep where she is contaminated with plutonium? Well, this was a similar experience. After a SWAT team assembled, I went through the x-ray machine (so much for pretending I didn't pack doughnuts) and was escorted to a small corral where more security personnel were loudly summoned and I was, publicly, FRISKED! Not wanded. FRISKED. Yes, I do feel that capitals are warranted in both sentences. This was extreme. I was HANDLED. In PUBLIC. They touched my ASS. I think I am getting my point across. My ass was in no way a weapon of mass destruction.

We think there is a very clear lesson to be learned here for B-FAB travelers everywhere. Unbeknownst to the general public, unreported by the media, there must be a big run on chunky white women letting their driver's licenses expire and then becoming airport threats. Who knew? I was, clearly, a victim of profiling. Don't let that happen to you or your ass. Whenever you travel make sure you have a CURRENT (I'm really into this caps thing but don't worry—it will pass) ID. Again, make sure you have a CURRENT (couldn't resist) driver's license or passport. Follow all the rules and above all, pack your own snacks; that airport food is nasty.

Pooling Around at the Holiday Inn

LB: Co-Founding Member Confessional

I compulsively obsess over everything. This is actually a redundant concept that obsesses upon itself. Yes indeed I, Laura Banks, am neurotic over life's tiniest details, only finding moments of peace inside various activities like: defuzzing sweaters, watching the Weather Channel, crying like a small child, or inhaling an entire warm wheel of Brie cheese in one sitting.

Sometimes I find myself obsessing about the good days of times gone by. Some of my few happy memories from my childhood are those of road trips and motels. As a kid I used to love trips, with the family car stocked with a Styrofoam cooler of food and us finally landing at my favorite place in the world, the Holiday Inn. I particularly loved the neon sign leading our family from the darkness toward the light; like a near-death ex-

perience we moved toward the blue light . . . coming from . . .
the swimming pool.

Mom would pack a giant cooler full of sandwiches and Cokes
and when that ran out—about an hour into the trip—we'd stop
at an A&W Root Beer drive-thru or a McDonald's or some
great diner along the way. I always remember wondering to
myself, Why didn't Mom pack more sandwiches? The cooler
always emptied way too fast. My ever-hungry brothers would
always sneak into the ice chest while I was napping—devouring
my entire tuna on white bread sandwich and my small, private
sack of Lay's potato chips. How come sometimes the sandwiches
aren't wrapped right and they get all mushy from the ice? Why
didn't my mom write my name on a napkin and wrap it around
my sandwich? How could she be so thoughtless? Doesn't she
know, other than swimming, that this is one of the most important parts of the trip? I have such issues with my mother.

We'd drive in the packed family car for what seemed like
eternity. (With three kids in the back of an Oldsmobile, five
family members was exactly the wrong number for someone as
tall as me to be comfortable.) Car bingo helped to pass the time.
Day would finally give in to night on the open highway. Fire-
flies would come out—dusk was teeming with possibility.

When I'd catch my first glimpse of the hotel sign from the
backseat of the family car I was unbelievably happy. After we
checked into our room there were many things to get done; I
had to unwrap soaps, pull off the strip of paper from the toilet
seat, and find the soda and ice machine outside. But the most
exciting, the most important, the most awesome part of the
trip . . . was the blue-lit-diving-board-deep-end-swimming pool.
The plan was always the same: Get into my bathing suit as soon
as I checked in. Force my way into the bathroom before any-

one else, throw on my suit, grab a towel, and head toward the pool. I'd run so fast to the pool that my towel would slip off my half-formed, mutant girl body. Squishy private parts and funny, bumpy things were forming, seemingly emerging in my sleep. I had the timing of an adolescent, awkward and out of rhythm. I was always tugging at my suit, pulling it out from my tiny butt crack. I'd always grab the towel and move it back and forth from my shoulders to my ass, back to my shoulders, then back to my waist to hide my legs. I had mixed emotions about my suit. I loved it because it was my costume that got me in the pool, but I also hated it because it exposed me—going through my awkward giant-tall-body stage.

I pressed on in the darkness toward the pool, often found beneath the glow of the famous giant sign. I'd open the little metal door. "Yippppee!" I'd dive, headfirst, into the deep end. (Getting in too deep and too fast became the theme of my life. See "D-List Boyfriend" confessional.) I would sing gleefully to myself, "I'm in the water!!" I was free of my ALV. In the magic of the blue waters I was free of my negative self-talk and doubts. I had escaped the embarrassment of my forming parts and my difficulties with my competitive brothers. Another big thing: I could also be shorter. I could stop obsessing over my funny-looking bottom, and button breasts. I escaped all my adolescent embarrassments in the water's velvety blue coolness. My hair became flat to the side of my head. I could make bubbles with my nose and I could . . . float. Once in the pool, I never, ever wanted to come out. (If I could live there, maybe be a mermaid, I'd never have to feel my weight again. I'd never have to figure out what clothes to put on to cover up my body ever, ever again for the rest of my life!)

But, alas, my ass would have to come out of the water and I'd have to find my way back to the hotel room, shivering the entire way. Sometimes I'd have to wait on the side of the bed all wet while my brothers or mom or dad spent way too much time in the bathroom. But it was worth it. All of it. Even that pebble that went into my foot on the barefoot walk home, even my wrinkly prune fingers were worth it. Yes, even peeling myself out of my cold, wet suit into my pajamas was part of the painful yet pleasurable experience. I had felt myself loving myself. I had sensed the weight of my youth leave me alone during those precious hours in the pool. Thank you Mom and Dad for great vacations. Thank you Holiday Inn for supplying a well-lighted pool—at decent discount prices. Thank you for my first out-of-body experience toward the light . . . and the great unknown.

Happy Holidass

hink of the holidays as an opportunity to be tortured by your whole family all at the same time. You can make it work for you. If you're new at embracing your Big Fat Ass, then we suggest that you not fight it. Submit to the horror of Thanksgiving and Christmas with your family. Holidays are the special times of year when you see all those family members you haven't seen since last year's festive season. That means you have to worry about how much you weighed last year compared to this year and have to contend with your aunt Midge making pointed comments about thin girls, like your cousin Angie, who are getting lots more marriage proposals. (She will say this to you even if you are on your third marriage.) Those magical, traditional holidays will always stay the same . . . with all the alcohol-induced cravings and ravings, childhood recriminations, fits and tantrums. On the upside you hardly even notice your crazy relatives because you're so busy stuffing yourself like you're pushing to become the lead float in the next Macy's Thanksgiving Day Parade. Erma Bombeck said it best: "I come from a family where gravy is considered a beverage."

Weight Watchers has emergency meetings before every holiday because they know we're going to be faced with mountains of munching. They also know we're emotional wrecks this time of year and that we use food to hide our utter sense of hopelessness and our lack of faith. (Just remember to keep smiling at all the parties.)

Magazines and TV shows spend lots of time before each frenetic festivity giving you coping strategies. Like, devour two cartons of cherry tomatoes before you go to that New Year's Eve party. But we think, Who on earth would want to go through a holiday without overeating? Isn't that what holidays are for? They are days that happen every year when we ritualistically get to "pig." Thanksgiving and Christmas are the heavy hitters. We'll start with those.

Hip-Hip-Hooray It's Thanksgiving Day

Thanksgiving is a holiday which we celebrate *entirely* by eating. This is no time to be messing around with any kind of diet. This is a B-FAB red-letter day. Wear black stretch pants. That's essential. That's your holiday uniform—best matched with an overblouse two sizes too big. Avoid giant turkey patches on your pockets. You'll look ridiculous.

Your problem may not be the appliqués, it could be the food.

Food you can't eat in secret and that your relatives will definitely criticize you about. You won't enjoy it nearly as much as if you were eating in the privacy of your own home with just your cat for company. Little Fluffy is much less judgmental than Great-Aunt Fluffy. Once you start eating you may not be able to stop. It's amazing how much stuffing you can stuff in your stomach if you just eat slowly—but not too slowly because you don't want your brain to realize you're not hungry anymore. The best game plan at Thanksgiving is to figure out your favorite foods and start with them in case you get so full you faint. Who wants to lose consciousness before the pumpkin pie?

Note: Avoid touch football in the backyard along with the raking of leaves. There is no reason to exercise at all—instead binge-eat out of boredom. We do. We love it. Plan several naps on Thanksgiving Day. You will need them because the turkey is filled with tryptophan, which makes you sleepy. When you wake up you can justify scarfing back a plate of leftovers just to get you through to your next lie-down.

Happy Ho-Ho

By the time you get to Christmas your eating frenzy has gained control and you've given up the fight. Now you are in a position to really make a difference. The excuse "But it's Christmas!" can cover a lot of rum balls. It's the most stressful time of year for dysfunctional families (see the JB confessional "Christmas Eve Chronicle"). Overeating has always worked in the past to make the holidays easier—we say if it ain't broke, don't fix it. It's a good idea to start every day of the season with a few glasses of wine so you can forget how tight your pants are (unless you have on those stretch pants, which is really the best approach: the oversized ones you bought at Thanksgiving).

December has another added bonus: you're broke because you bought presents for everybody in the free world. B-FAB Janette does it differently. She loves Christmas shopping and has to make many, many trips to the stores. That's because she often comes home with two bags of lovely things for herself, having completely forgotten to pick up the golf club sock for Uncle Donny, which was really the whole reason she had gone shopping in the first place.

Christmas is also very expensive for many of us because we have to add extra therapy sessions. In general, although not exclusively, Christmas is a time to spend quality time with the ungodly, annoying family members whose covert, critical projections made you fat in the first place. Go ahead. Suck back that incredible Williams-Sonoma chocolate-and-caramel-covered giant Fuji apple. It will help. Yes it will. You can go on a diet in January with everybody else—not that it will work any better this year than it did last.

The Last Temptation of Halloween

Halloween is the most important of the secondary holidays that occur within the eating season—which starts on October 31 and ends on January 1, give or take two weeks of leftovers. When you feel fat and candy is everywhere it's impossible to resist and eating it makes you feel miserable about yourself. No matter where you turn: candy corn. (Have you noticed that no one in the world admits to actually buying candy corn and yet it's always everywhere? Isn't that odd?) You can't go into any store at all without being confronted by piles and shelves and bins of sweets. There will be bowls of the stuff where you work. Your skinny ass coworkers will bring in buckets of excess candy and plant it, like land mines, all around the office. You're screwed. We've gotten the same subliminal Halloween message since childhood: Eat candy. Get fat. Get lots of cavities. (It's fun. We've tried it.)

Halloween is also the time of year when some of your friends think it would be fun for grown-up adults to go out dressed as Queen Elizabeth or Jack Sparrow. Some people may feel that it's bad enough to be fat without being a fat pirate with a patch. Try to see the positive side. You can get possessed by the spirit of some dead lady from the nineteenth century—pretend that your ass and thighs are a bustle.

Halloween isn't for everyone. If you fit in this category, a great way to get through the holiday is to turn off all the lights and hide in the walk-in closet if anyone comes. Is that normal? Of course it is. *Anything* is normal for a B-FAB sister!

Valentine's Day—A Time for Suffering

If you're sitting home alone on V-Day, just crack open a bottle of Baileys Irish Cream and remember every bad date you ever had. Don't omit the time your boyfriend needled and needled you to help him pick out something inexpensive for your room-mate's birthday and then instead he gave it to you on Valentine's Day. (That was That Asshole Todd—see the JB confessional.) These things happen to everyone. Don't blame your ass. Blame men. All of them.

There is way too much pressure on women everywhere on

Valentine's Day. If there is one day a year where you really should allow yourself to binge like a snorker, it's the big V-Day. Take yourself out to dinner. Get drunk. Food is a great cure for loneliness. Food can be your date! Let's face it: a box of bon-bons fills you up like no man can. Even if by some miracle you have something that passes for a relationship on the Foul Four-teenth (as we affectionately call it) there is still too much ex-pectation to actually be happy on this holiday. Everything on V-Day has to be bigger and better than any other day of the year. Last February Janette got a fax about buying roses. Where it came from we do not know, but it was a "Special Valentines Offer!" They were selling Super-Roses! Bigger Roses! Better Roses! (Is this so your ass will look smaller by comparison?) This is how we discovered that getting plain old roses is no longer enough. Here's what we suggest: If this is your first Valentine's Day with a new boyfriend, you better hope he starts with a bud in a vase so he has room to grow. Otherwise by the time you've been together for ten years he'll have to just get a cauliflower and paint it red.

Valentine's Day is the day that you're supposed to wear red. Okay, but only on top. Never wear those matching mono-chromatic tops and bottoms. You'll look like a caboose. Don't get carried away with those lacy, patterned blouses and skirts, either. People will think you're Omar the Tentmaker. No mat-ter how many of your friends say you look fetching in that circle skirt covered with appliqué hearts, shrug them off! They are lying to you. You look horrible in it. People will think there's a circus going on under there or maybe a hideout for a litter of kittens, or worse yet, they'll think it's your *Ass*.

Valentine's Day is the only day of the year when you can acceptably buy underwear for someone else. When it's a cowork-er's birthday, for instance, you don't immediately leap to "I'll bet she'll like Jockeys—all cotton!" When the receptionist re-tires from your doctor's office after fifty years you don't go "I'll get her a thong!" However, see-thru teddies, push-up bras, and feathered anything are not a great gift choice for most B-FABs. Our men love us just as we are. They think we look great in skimpy underwear but we're horrified that they'll want us to pole-dance around with our cellulite hanging out. We say, "Don't do it!" Put on some pink long johns and a big shirt and enjoy the holiday. Pay him back by buying him boxer shorts with hearts on them. (Make him dance.) How romantic is that? He takes off his jeans and he looks like Bozo.

Presidents' Day—Go Buy Some Sheets

Finally, a holiday that isn't about food. It also doesn't have any annoying family obligations. It's a day off from work. Paid. Which brings us to why this is still a very important holiday for B-FABs: it spells SALES! We're not sure how we honor famous dead presidents by shopping but it's okay with us. Lincoln had a day-bed sale at Jennifer Convertible. What's better than Calvin Coolidge day at Kohl's? Need some wooden teeth? We're sure George has a sale day coming up. These presidents kicking the bucket and creating marketing opportunities also give B-FABs a great chance to be compulsive about something other than food. It's hard to eat Cheetos while fighting older, frailer women to get the sheets with the best thread count.

Fourth of July—Beyond Sparklers

The Fourth is a challenge for most B-FABs because it includes the dreaded "family barbecue." You will be faced with potato salad, hot dogs, burgers, and your fat aunt Martha. You will feel pressure to eat. We recommend you go ahead. Use both hands. The next hurdle is finding a cool enough summer outfit that doesn't make you look like headcheese. (That's not real cheese—it's made from the meat off the head of a calf or pig that is seasoned, combined with a gelatinous meat broth, and cooked in a mold. Basically, it's lumpy face of pig. It looks like cellulite. Yum.) Shorts are often problematical . . . what with the red, white, and blue chafing of your inner thighs. The Fourth of July is a time to show how patriotic you are by tattooing the American flag on your backside. Depending on the size of your BFA, you might want to include state flags as well. (Not including Alaska.) This is a holiday we can enjoy. It's all about the fireworks . . . not looking at your ass.

We're pretty sure that people import extra mosquitoes for these parties, so no matter what you wear you will have the added attraction of scabby arms and legs and constant scratching. (You may have thoughtful and incisive questions, like "If they suck enough blood will I weigh less?") Nothing is more entertaining for others than watching you try to surreptitiously scratch the bite in the middle of your left butt cheek. We recommend using the salad fork or a sparkler. If you don't have one, just borrow from your host. Even a firecracker can do the trick.

But Wait, There's More

Those are all the major eating holidays that we can think of. We know there are lots of little ones—Groundhog Day, Bastille Day, or Cinco de Mayo. Start thinking these up yourself. Why do we have to do all the work? Make them real celebrations where you can take time off from criticizing and depriving yourself. Go ahead. Act just as if you were a normal person! Eat that bacon cheeseburger and swill beer straight out of the keg. Then stop. Never underestimate the truth of Cyndi Lauper's anthem: "Girls Just Want to Have Fun." Well—so do B-FABs!

Christmas Eve Chronicle

JB: Co-Founding Member Confessional

s a compulsive overeater I can say, with quite a lot of certainty, and after years of therapy, that I eat to avoid things. That's why the holidays are *such* a challenging time for people with food issues. With both massive amounts of food and all those relatives around there is so much to avoid! Below you will find a timeline of one of my festive family celebrations. I'm pretty sure I gained six pounds in three days that year. It's okay. I needed to.

December 24

1:00 PM
My father is walking around my sister's house pointing out specks. "There's a little black thing on the floor over there.

There's something on your shirt. What's that on your shoe?" My sister didn't answer. Instead she walked into the kitchen and yelled back, "I forgot what I came in here for. Does anybody know?"

1:15 PM

I'm wondering if I should tell sister that her hair is scary. When she came out of the bathroom I did mention that it kind of looked like a beehive. She didn't cover her head, scream, and run like I would have done so I assume she's all right with it and I should keep my mouth shut.

My father is his usual holiday self. He's telling us that the Christmas cards this year were awful, *and* they want three or four dollars for them. Oh, they had some for ninety-nine cents—"Course that's a dollar"—but they looked too cheap to send. None of them had verses on them that were worth anything.

3:00 PM

My sister gets so horrified while my father's driving that her voice gets calm and deliberate like she's talking to a mental patient. This makes him so nervous he twitches and swerves all over the place. Me, I'm scared in any car no matter who's driving. So, to celebrate the holiday, we went for a drive.

This is an ordeal. Go to the store with a seventy-eight-year-old with a bad knee. Go ahead. My father insisted on driving his car so the first thing he does is to try to rearrange all the junk on the floor. He delivered the warnings: don't slip on this catalog;

watch out for that bag; be careful of the paper towels. Then he drove into the street over the curb. ("Damn thing—why do they put those there?")

4:05 PM

Sitting at Colonial Times—a restaurant with a bar that my sister, Lanette, likes. They were having a special Christmas happy hour. I didn't think it would be a good time to mention that I would rather shoot myself through the head than go to happy hour. The bartender had Lanette's drink made for her before she even took off her coat. She didn't seem to realize that that is not a good sign.

Father's comments about the cappuccino: "The cups aren't very big. How much do they charge for that? Will they give you a refill?"

4:40 PM

Leaving Colonial Times, Lanette insisted on giving us a tour of the Christmas lights outside the restaurant even though it was still daylight and they weren't turned on. She insisted we exit the far door so we could walk the entire distance around the restaurant in the freezing, biting, these-chenille-pants-aren't-really-warm-enough cold while she pointed out wires on bushes.

[Back in the Car]

Father: How much were those drinks?

Lanette: The cocktails?

Father: Yes.

Lanette: Six dollars I guess.

Father: You don't know for sure?

Lanette: I don't remember the price of every single thing.

Father: When I was young they were a quarter.

Lanette: Well, wouldn't that be nice.

[Still driving]

Father: Damn those cars all coming up on me just when I have to get over to that lane.

Me: Where? Which way do you have to go?

Lanette: He's fine right here. He doesn't have to go anywhere right now. That's the fast lane.

Father: Well I'm going to go over as soon as I can. The hell with 'em.

[Squealing tires and blaring horn. Now in the left lane.]

7:00 PM

[Conversation guaranteed to put one in the Christmas spirit]

Father: Seems as though it was just yesterday that you were little girls. And you can't even really say you're middle-aged now because no one ever really lives to be a hundred.

We said we'd rather talk about something else on Christmas Eve. Lanette suggested her vegetable soup as a topic. I said maybe we could go one more. There has to be something better to talk about on a festive Christmas Eve than our own death or boiled roots.

Father: Time marches on. It waits for no man.

9:30 PM

Father: Life is going by. Every tick of the clock. Tick tock, tick tock.

10:15 PM

Father is asleep and Lanette and I are splitting a bottle of tequila. Holiday's not so bad after all! Where are the cookies? I bet there's brownies. Wow, I feel better already. Maybe Lanette made those incredible coconut and chocolate chip square things she makes. Maybe she'll surprise me with a Tunnel of Fudge cake! Who gives a crap about the size of my ass, where's the eggnog?

Now my father is living in a dementia unit. Whoever thought I would live to miss those crazy holiday conversations. We still see him at Christmas although he won't know it's Christmas. He does still point out specks. My sister no longer wears a beehive.

In Conclusion:
The Art of Masstery

Let's face it—there are no shortcuts to enlightenment. This book has given you multiple stories and images using the analogy of the ass, to illustrate how and where in life we hold ourselves back. We want you to know that you have been holding back on your greatness, sitting on it, repressing it for some time now. Know that for the most part your constant inner chatter and perfectionism and comparing yourself to others has basically cost you your life. It's time to stop being cheap and stingy when it comes to expressing self-love. Give up some of those old stories. You are one fabulous fat ass babe with millions of wonderful thoughts and feelings to share with yourself and your pets. (Okay, you can include the world.)

Let's go back in time to another era. Is *zaftig* just a big word for "fat"? Marilyn Monroe was a size fourteen—fat by current standards—and is considered today to be one of the most beautiful women that has ever walked the earth. She was hot! If she was a starlet in Hollywood now, nobody would hire her. They'd send her home to go on the Cayenne Pepper diet first. What happened in the last thirty or forty years that created the downfall of the curve? Elizabeth Taylor, Jayne Mansfield, Jane Russell, Mae West, and Sophia Loren—these are no slouches.

The ideal size fluctuates from generation to generation; previous to the zaftig era was the flapper era, when, like today, women had to look like Angelina Jolie. Okay, it's just history, but history can suck—take for instance the Roman Colosseum or the Plague. What's a girl to do? We offer up this defense mechanism: the next time someone suggests you go on a diet, look them straight in the eye and reply, "No thanks, I'm emulating another era—one when women were women, and men were men, and bras were designed to work like battleships."

Let's be there for each other to yell and cheer as we cross the finish line of new successes in our personal relationships, at work and even with our underpants. Your first goal after finishing this book and going on our B-Fabulous website is to create your very own fan club for *yourself*. Find coaches, friends, surrogates, and loved ones who won't judge you, who get you at the fat ass core of who you are.

Of course you can always choose to be by yourself like the Lone Ranger or the Bionic Woman. Please take note: people who need to play the hero are often alone, give or take a sidekick. (It works the same for villains: Catwoman roamed back alleys in search of a saucer of milk. Got milk?) Please, don't disappear in a masquerade of loner low self-esteem. Take off that perfectionist's Wonder Woman cape and come be real with us.

(Capes often get in the way. You can trip on them while leaping tall buildings . . . and the dry cleaning bill is horrendous.)

Be joyful in numbers. Find us and we will find you and we will help you find yourself as we find ourselves. (Huh! What did she just say?) Get a life. Boldly go where no big ass has gone before. Know that change, change toward having a great life with a great big ass takes patience . . . and Preparation H. Hire an administrative assistant to manage your fat ass and all the crazy bookkeeping and number crunching that goes on around it in your head. You are the business owner of this fine establishment called You and it's time to get on with having an extraordinary life! Travel. Fall in love. Shake it up in a hula hoop. Nobody is better than you and we will tell you that every day if you let us. Watch our blog. Visit our blog. (We wish they had invented another name for such a far-reaching cultural phenomena. A *blog*? Please.)

Your future is waiting. Forget your past and leave it in your pants. We're here for you through fat or thin. E-mail us your story about how you have overcome your ass, or how it's overcome you on occasion. We'll share it with others and they will say, "Oh my God, that happened to me, too!" By coming together we can get you off that deserted island called You. We've informed the Coast Guard.

And there you go. And there we go. And we've got to go. We have absolutely nothing left to share about our ass except for everything we haven't said yet. Carpe diem, live long and prosper, and . . . YABBA-DABBA-DOOOOOOO!!!!

The Asstrological Reader

s we go out into the world embracing our BFAs there are many other unseen forces at play. One of the great mysteries of life is that not only is B-FAB Laura a writer who's learned to embrace every inch of herself, she's also an astrologer. Laura's mother was a great astrologer, as was her aunt Gloria on her mother's side. (Surprise, we bet you didn't think Laura was going to say anything nice about her mother before the end of the book.) They say psychic gifts run in the family. Laura does wear bangs to hide that third eye in the middle of her forehead.

Planetary transits and forecasts are determined by their positions in the sky at any given time. This science of the sky has been around for more than five thousand years. If you've never picked up *Cosmo's Bedside Astrologer* and you have no idea what your sun sign is, where the hell have you been? Albert Einstein believed in the power of astrology, as have presidents and heads of state. In this chapter we'll discuss sun signs and how they relate back to your big dipper of a bottom, along with every other esoteric concept we could configure.

Aries: The Ram (March 21–April 20)

Aries love to play. Throw them in a sandbox and watch them build a glass bottling company. One of our two noble and trusted leaders in the B-FAB movement is an Aries, our very own sister goddess Laura Banks. When it comes to loving herself and putting herself above all others, she embodies the kill-everyone-and-leave-no-enemies approach to life. Her planet, Mars, is the sign of war. Like any good army sergeant she keeps herself from bemoaning the numbers on the scale any given morning by keeping really, really busy. Aries is the master of the "to-do" list. Ram chicks and chippies are whirlwinds of movement, often reducing the size of their ass by, like hummingbirds, never sitting anywhere for more than a few seconds. They have the attention span of a gnat, so if you're speaking to them you'd better make it fast.

What is an Aries' favorite food? Appetizers. It comes first. If for some godawful reason she is forced to wait willy-nilly to actually eat with other guests, she can get pretty pissed. It's not an Aries' fault if the rest of the zodiac is late for supper. If an Aries babe eats enough off the nacho platter at Chili's, she is likely to excuse herself from the main course and never come back to the table. One minute she's sitting there, the next she's off taking a nice jog around the mall. While running she may, oh, we don't know, think up a cure for cancer. (Of course, Cancers are born in July.)

Taurus: The Bull (April 21–May 20)

Taurean femmes tend to put on weight faster than Janet Jackson. We are not sure exactly why, but we think it has something to do with eating. Lots and lots of eating. When you are a Taurus, food is the most glorious thing on the planet. That's because Taureans are homey-cozy folk. A Taurean bull chick can eat nothing but a Ritz cracker and put on a pound—if a wind blows in the wrong direction, another five pounds. A Taurus can be upwards of ten to twenty feet from the kitchen and, if someone is cooking comfort food, she can jump up from her Buddha Bull position and be upright over the dish with a fork in less than five seconds. Then she brushes back her flaring nostrils and returns to human form, gives one of her winning, feminine smiles, and proceeds to eat like a horse without the feedbag.

You may be thinking, Thank God I'm not a Taurus. You may even be pitying these poor bull chicks right now. Cut it out. You are not immune to the influence of this fixed constellation. You may have Taurus Moon sign or Taurus Rising sign, which you can only figure out by doing a full chart reading. We all use food to try to gain control of many issues in our lives and, what could be more shocking, it doesn't work.

Gemini: The Twins (May 21–June 21)

Being the master communicators of the Zodiass (pronounced: "zode-ee-ass") with their ruling planet represented by the

winged gent himself, Mercury, Geminis are human thermome-
ters. How a Gemini Thinks: I find you attractive. Do you find
me attractive? Do you come here often? May I have my way
with your boyfriend?

Twin chicks intuitively time their every move and always
know when to pounce. The thermostat can run hot and cold
with their dual personalities—one minute they're planning to
leave a party, the next they change their minds and decide to
start singing karaoke. Geminis are so endearing that that schizo-
phrenic thing doesn't really even bother you. They're not at the
party, they *are* the party. They have a permanent party going on
in their heads—equal to about ten people, but not to worry
about the buffet. Since they are bigger talkers than eaters,
they'll cut down on your catering bill. Remember, the Twins
can pull off eating and talking at the same time. In fact, they
can hold their own with two of anything at the same time:
two conversations, two cupcakes, or two people. (Take this any
way you want. It's your fantasy.)

When it comes to issues of self-worth or self-loathing, it de-
pends on which of her personalities you're talking to. For the
most part, the chasm in a Gemini's mind lends itself more toward confusion than self-hatred. Geminininians like to keep it
light so any kind of introspection is out of the question. They
don't bother with things that aren't fun. And isn't that great?
We all could learn from this playful pioneer and create more
fun, play, and ease in our own lives.

Cancer: The Crab (June 22–July 22)

We love these gals because what you see is what you get: fat 'n'
crabby. The moon with all its waxing and waning will usually

have its way with a Cancerian soul. The weight of a Cancer, like the tides of the ocean, will fluctuate like a blowfish. If you are Cancer you are moody and in search of distraction—usually in the form of comfort food and digestibles like mashed potatoes, roasted meats, and fried chicken. Cancerians inspire us all to greater heights or depths, or spreads. Whatever.

The advantage of being a Cancer is that you are a natural homemaker. When you are not busy being a curmudgeon, you *love* nurturing yourself, others, and the planet. Cancer chicks are usually consumed with managing the affairs of others, which is their escape from the dilemma of their ass. You could benefit from putting two relationships first before all others—your relationship with your kitchen and your therapist.

Leo: The Lion (July 23–August 22)

Leo is the king of the jungle, the color gold, and master of the multiple uses of MasterCard. Shopping is a great diversion from any physical flaws found in their flubby behinds. Meals in the lioness's home should be served on gold plates with lots of sauces followed by desserts that catch on fire. Being waited on hand and foot in trendy restaurants is how Leos like to feed their BFAs. They also like to look at very beautiful people while eating, so be sure to take them to some trendy eateries . . . like Hooters. (We hear the chicken wings are really good.)

Leos have huge appetites but they are often lucky enough for all that fat to spread kind of evenly over their big golden bods. They probably have an entourage. If you are lucky enough to get a seat next to a Leo at a dinner party or a restaurant you will receive royal service by proxy. Waiters and waitresses will naturally gravitate to fill your water or wine glass first, clear your plate, or sit on your lap. Enjoy the view.

Virgo: The Virgin (August 23–September 23)

Too nervous to eat? Concerned about germs or whether you are allergic to something in the sauce? Welcome to the world of Virgo. Virgos get their BFAs thanks to what we can safely call "nervous eating." The average Virgo will be calculating the exact total of the check as she anxiously puts a tiny taste of something on the tip of her tongue. Here are some of the things a Virgo may be thinking:

✧ Did I remember to clean the kitty litter?

✧ Did I forget to have sex with my husband this morning?

✧ How do I get out of this bathroom without touching this doorknob?

✧ I need more Post-its.

On a more positive note, these Virgin members are natural healers with highly refined manners and a surprising sense of humor. They are an earth sign, but unlike their other earth sign friends (Capricorn and Taurus), for some reason these guys escaped the Big Bang with a dry wit. This eases their nerves and wins over so many fans. And your natural understanding of your body and health can often make you the best friend to have— teaching all of us which foods to eat and which to shove off onto your pet turtle. Thanks, Virg.

Libra: The Scales (September 23–October 22)

Libra is the seventh sign of the zodiac. The number seven represents relationships. It is opposite the willful sign Aries, which is all about me, me, and me. Combined, these two can soar to fabulous heights. Librans have an uncanny ability to put others to work. Librans are coy and flirtatious powerhouses. They can convince complete strangers to take out the trash, repaint the bathroom, or marry them. They don't like heavy lifting and straining. They are very good at sitting. That's why so many Librans have such gorgeous BFAs. Our lovely and talented sister goddess Janette is a Libra. She balances out the more impulsive personality of Fat Ass Co-Founding Member Ram chick Laura. Thank goodness for friends like this. Together they make one complete and somewhat normal person.

If you are planning to throw a dinner party, we highly recommend that you invite one of these engaging Libra B-FABs to your party. The battle cry of this Venusian babe is "Everyone please bring a dish or two." Before you know it the table is brimming with food and you'll think the Babe-of-All-Things-Fair-and-Balanced cooked all the dishes herself. She'll conveniently hide the leftovers in the back of her fridge for late-night snacking when everyone has finally gone home and left the poor girl alone.

Scorpio: The Scorpion (October 23–November 22)

Scorpio represents the number eight because it's the eighth sign in the zodiac. What a stretch. Taken literally, there is an upper and a lower hemisphere to the digit itself and a Scorpio BFA exists in one of those two hemispheres. They either soar like eagles or crawl around and hide under rocks like lizards. That's what makes it the most misunderstood sun sign of the zodiac. These she-devils have unbelievable cravings—passions that come from living in survival mode. This is the most possessive sign and if they have you in their sights for any reason, you're dead meat. Remember, their symbol is the scorpion. Now, there is a critter not to mess with.

They can emotionally "eat" their dates and spouses. Scorpios devour you with their piercing stare, sucking you down to the bone. Most Scorpio sun signs are more ravenous for sensual pleasures than food. They'll consider kissing an appetizer and making love as the entrée. Any dish that is difficult to obtain and serve is of interest—clams on a half shell, escargot, sushi, really any small, crying creatures. Drop a live lobster into a pot—they love to listen to it scream. Scorpio loves anything with sauces, secret recipes, and alcohol. This helps loosen up an otherwise stone-faced gal. Get her really liquored up to find out who she's dating and what secret weight loss program she's been on to shed unwanted pounds. In truth, if you are lucky enough to land a Scorpio in your life, know that no matter what they will always love you until they don't anymore. These gals are psychic—ask them your lotto-ball numbers or which guy you should start to get more serious about.

Sagittarius: The Archer
(November 22–December 20)

If you are born under this sign you are a happy-go-lucky gal born with Jupiter as your ruling planet. You love to travel, laugh, philosophize, and eat. You have a rock star mentality along with the luck of a leprechaun. Your motto is "You can't hit a moving target." Come on baby let the good times roll as you take on higher education, belief systems, and life's big adventures. Cruise ship buffets are your forte and you laugh your way to the front of the line, mounding every single entrée available onto your plate all at once.

The possibility of enlarging upon their Big Fat Asses is a concern for this sign because Sagittarians have no problem eating . . . anywhere, anytime, with any passing tourist. B-FABs can stay in check with this simple trick: the next time you're out at a B-FAB Society function, put a Post-it on your friend's head that reads "Don't forget, you're eating." The other good news with Sagittarians is that they are fire signs, so they naturally burn a fair amount of calories just by spewing their latest concepts on eternal happiness.

Capricorn: The Goat (December 21–January 19)

Being born under the sign of the billy goat makes for a very practical personality. You like to build things: tables, chairs, businesses, and BFAs. Your element is earth—your asses can become masses and be rock solid. Capricorns are stoic and grounded. Your legs may resemble table legs but you can solve that by wearing pants. Bell-bottoms are a good choice.

Breakfast, lunch, and dinner are the cornerstones of your day-to-day existence. You like to use meals to figure out what time it is. Unlike Leos or Sagittarians, Cap babes don't need to be with other people to enjoy eating. They can dine all by themselves and savor every last morsel. She-goats live in their minds, on the side of cliffs in remote corners of the world, making for not the most social of folks. (You can sometimes find them in the upper bedroom eating their meals on their laps while playing with the house puppy.)

On the rare occasion when you do meet a Cap chick at a dinner party, consider yourself lucky; get all the information on anything you can out of them because they are usually Big Fat Ass know-it-alls. (The older signs are at the end of the zodiac. Sagittarius, Capricorn, Aquarius, and Pisces are considered more universal so they absorb information like sponges.) Ask a Cap anything—how to whip up the perfect meringue, make curtains, or build a bookstore.

Aquarius: The Water Bearer
(January 22–February 18)

Aquarians are air signs—the true brain waves of the zodiac. They could be breatharians (which are people that live off of air somewhere in California). Aquarius is one of the signs least interested in food, and Aquarians are often quite thin yet they could care less what they look like. They'd rather everybody just get along and live in peace, damn it. When they're not out trying to save the planet, they prefer to eat organic food while singing "Kumbaya." No one likes someone who sings with their mouth full. While dining out, Aquarius is most likely to be lost in thought mulling over questions like:

1. Is the "waitperson" being paid more than the minimum wage?

2. Did the main course once roam the earth?

3. Dessert? No thank you. Did I remember to buy tickets to Sting's next fund-raiser?

Aquarians don't eat ham sandwiches. They know too much about how pigs suffer slow, grisly deaths in meatpacking plants. They swore off eating anything with a face years ago. Favored foods: nuts, seeds, vegan burgers, salads, whole grain breads, and drugs of all kinds. Yes, drugs. Unfortunately or fortunately, however you wish to look at it, this sign enjoys altered states of consciousness. Unlike many of the rest of the signs, they like to get high not to forget about their enlarging waistline so much as to forget about the shrinking ionosphere. These are great B-FABs to have around because they get your mind off your ass in short order. One minute you're obsessing over the size of your hips, then an Aquarian babe gets your head out of your ass by taking you to a local rally in town to save the Mexican beetle. (That was the original drummer for the Beatles.)

Pisces: The Fish (February 19–March 20)

The final celestial sign of the zodiac is the illusive B-FAB Pisces. (You didn't know you could be illusive with a Big Fat Ass, did you? But even this late in the book we are still here to tell you that anything is possible.) Pisces is the sign of the fish, so keep in mind you can eat them. Neptunian Pisces are so busy taking care of others' emotional wreckage that they often have nothing left for themselves. Keep in mind these are great friends to get ahold of when you want to rant about your sorry boyfriend. They can channel anything and everything, which leads to mental confusion. Fortunately for these oceanic B-FABs, there are things you can do to make yourself feel better. Disconnect your phone. Live near the water; it will bring you peace and maybe a man with a boat. Do not eat to disguise the complexity of your emotions. Get a good shrink.

Anyway, thanks to Pisces for being the last sign on the zodiac and for taking on all human suffering. Enjoy some delicious herbal teas and cakes with friends today. Take in a play. Do something sensual to get out of your karma, maybe go swimming or eat a Bundt cake. Do whatever it takes, for God's sake, but don't go it alone. Successful fish swim in packs, like Charlie the Tuna.

Acknowledgments
(in alphabetical order)

To All the Fabulous Women who contributed testimonials, we want to thank you for your courage to come forward in this book. We also want to thank Stewart Banks for all your stories and encouragement and Richard Banks for being a great brother. To Gwendolyn Banks, thanks for being a highly creative and loving mother. We appreciate Lanette Barber, brilliant artist and metalsmith, for shouldering the impossible task of being Janette's sister. We're beyond grateful to Barry Brown, the perfect boyfriend, for all your trips to the copier, post office, and FedEx, not to mention grocery shopping for our long writing sessions up at the house. To Fran Capo, thanks for assuring us that we weren't insane. Our literary agent Adam Chromy we salute for believing in us and for your brilliant strategies. Thank you, Janis Donnaud, for your integrity and friendship. We're grateful to Sophie Farargo for being the best cheerleader in the universe. Lisa Gold and Tony Nation, thanks for your ongoing support and generosity in letting us tape at Actors Connection. We also thank Daniel Nisbeth, the other perfect boyfriend, for your constant support and love, and Sara Nisbeth for your great tip on how to pull up your pants. We are so appreciative of you, Rosie O'Donnell, for your spectacular foreword and for being a constant inspiration. Thanks, Gina Otto, for being an angel, Suzanne O'Neill, our editor, for your tireless commitment to getting it right, and to Tom Pitoniak, our copy editor, for making us look smart. Dr. Alan Pressman for your eternal guidance and fabulous sense of humor. Carol Weidanthal, we are forever indebted to you for inspiring us by being the first one to embrace your Big Fat Ass. We tip our hats to Susan Winter, dear friend and brilliant author. And finally, to Michelle Wolfson for your work as our literary agent and for holding our hand for a year and a half, and being there whenever we needed you.

We could not have written this book without any of you and again, we really, really, really, really thank you.

Janette and Laura

New York, NY
January 3, 2008